MORE DIRECT BOOKINGS

ADAM HAMADACHE

First published in 2015 by Wow Guest Hotel Marketing (www.wowhotelmarketing.com)

© Copyright Adam Hamadache

All rights reserved. No part of this publication may be reproduced, stored in or introduced into a retrieval system, or transmitted, in any form, or by any means (electronic, mechanical, photocopying, recording or otherwise) without the prior written permission of the publisher.

This book is sold subject to the condition that it shall not, by way of trade or otherwise, be lent, resold, hired out, or otherwise circulated without the publisher's prior consent in any form of binding or cover other than that in which it is published and without a similar condition including this condition being imposed on the subsequent purchaser.

Front cover design by Sharon Larder
inthedoghousedesign@gmail.com

Dedicated to these wonderful, supportive people.

You've all played a huge role, in your own way, to my success. Whether I've come willingly, or you've dragged me kicking and screaming, you've helped me get where I am today. I'm eternally grateful to have, and to have had you in my life. Thank you.

Margaret, Louis, Lynda, Stuart, Jack, Simon, Ed, Francis, Tom, James, Stephen, Richard, Kate, Lee, Lucinda, Siam, Yannis, Stuart, Gemma, Amy, Barney, Olivia, Hannah, Michael, Tim, Frances.

Connect with Adam

Email: Adam@wowguest.com

Twitter: @adamhamadache

Website: www.moredirectbookings.com
www.wowhotelmarketing.com
www.thecranleigh.com

"Adam provides up to date and easily digested practical tips to help Hotels grow their direct revenue. There is so much waffle when it comes to digital marketing advice, but the tips in this book get straight to the point and give easily achievable goals with great financial outcomes to those that embrace the advice given."

Steve Lowy - Founder umi Hotels

"Adam Hamadache manages to explain the real-life application of modern marketing concepts that others often only seem able to relate in abstract terms. "This book deserves the attention of anyone whose aim is to successfully grab the attention of potential customers."

Peter Hancock FIH MI,
Chief Executive, Pride of Britain Hotels.

A good practical approach to an often mis-understood and over used form of marketing . Adam gives clear and concise advocate help to make your marketing attempts more effective and help you see a return on your efforts.

Janice Gault, Chief Executive,
Northern Ireland Hotel Federation

TABLE OF CONTENTS

A Personal Note from Adam 8
Introduction 11
How to Use This Book 14
How Not to Use This Book 16
Why Only *Reading* This Book is a Waste of Time. 18
Part One 19
    Tracking Telephone Numbers 19
    Google Analytics 22
    Lead Magnets 26
    Email Auto-Responders 29
    Customer Relationship Management (CRM) System 33
    Lead Scoring 35
    Printed Newsletter 39
    Facebook Advertising 43
    Google Adwords 45
    Measuring Cost-Per-Lead (CPL) and Cost-Per-Sale (CPS) 47
    Google Remarketing / Facebook Retargeting 50
    Local Non-Resident Dining 54
    SEO Critical Improvements 57
    Call Answering Company 59
    Controlling What Goes On Your TripAdvisor Page 61
    Video 64
    Automated Birthday Emails 67
    Facebook Data Upload & Lookalike Audiences 71
Part Two: 18 things you need to know about email marketing 73
    Introduction 73
    1. Subject Line 75
    2. Dual Readership Path 78
    3. Database Segmentation 79
    4. Whom The Email Is Sent 'From' 84

   5. Whom The Email Is Sent 'To' 86
   6. Email Engagement Strategy 87
   7. Tracking Telephone Numbers 90
   8. Split Testing 91
   9. Unopened Re-Send 95
   10. Time of Delivery 97
   11. Multiple Follow-Up 99
   12. Multiple Calls to Actions 100
   13. Encourage Unsubscribes 101
   14. Pre-Header 103
   15. Design 105
   16. Plain Text Emails 107
   17. PS 109
   18. How to Avoid Spam Complaints 110
Part Three **112**
   Referral Postcards 112
   The Complete Hotel Marketing System 115
Summary & Conclusion **120**

A PERSONAL NOTE FROM ADAM

Dear fellow hotelier

In 2014, 96% of the business we achieved at the Cranleigh Boutique came to us through direct, zero-commission channels. Our average occupancy for the year hovered at 86% and our average nightly rate was substantially higher than our closest competitors (both in terms of location and quality).

How did we do it?

We invested time, money and effort into marketing our product better than our competitors market their hotels. We also made sure we never, ever miss a sales opportunity. Lastly we made sure that we have a strategy for maximising the lifetime value of a customer to our business.

Having an excellent product in an ideal location helps of course.

Now after 8 years of driving more business to independent hotels, including my own, I feel it's about time that the wider industry knew what I know and approached the selling of bedrooms like I do. The important point to make however is that achieving similar results to what we have done at The Cranleigh Boutique for the last couple of years, is not simply about the marketing tips and tricks and whizzy online tools that will be outlined in detail throughout this book.

Rather, **how you think about this problem** of reducing dependency of the OTAs and improving the profitability of your business will have far greater impact on the overall commercial success of your hotel.

For example, I've met hoteliers who say they don't have time to do the marketing of the hotel, but will happily sit and rant about TripAdvisor for 30 minutes if you call them up out of the blue. I'll hear hoteliers say things like 'Facebook isn't for us' or 'we only send 3 emails per year as we don't want to bombard our customers'.

These types of behaviours and attitudes are why most hotels will never achieve the level of success we have at the Cranleigh. And, given you have bought this book, I'm assuming that you are ready to learn how to reduce your dependency of the OTAs. As such, please bear these three statements in mind:

    a) TripAdvisor is a business tool you must embrace, irrespective of the pain and frustration it might cause you
    b) Adults on the whole spend an average of 40+ minutes on Facebook everyday. Or to put another way – your customers are on Facebook right now. Choose to ignore this incontrovertible fact at your peril.
    c) Email is the most successful medium we have for driving new business: the more emails we send, the more business we achieve.

In my office, a plaque sits above my desk with a quote that reads as follows:

The problem is not the problem. The problem is your attitude about the problem.
- Captain Jack Sparrow

Wisdom, it emerges can be found in the most bizarre of places! These two sentences have helped me to think differently about the problem we all face as hoteliers, and without question this approach, combined with proven marketing techniques have yielded substantial returns.

So, with this in mind, I welcome you to embrace the concepts in this book, even if the suggestions don't sit with you comfortably at first. They will seem strange, even borderline radical at first but rest assured, they have worked for dozens of hotels just like yours.

Now, let's beat those OTAs together.

Adam
Associate Director, The Cranleigh Boutique
Founding Director, Wow Guest Hotel Marketing

INTRODUCTION

It's my view that hotels operate somewhat differently than most other businesses. Specifically, independent hotels operate differently. I'm referring to the way in which businesses get and keep customers. After all, what is more important than a business's ability to continually get and keep customers? Sure, if there are staffing problems or cash flow challenges or any other issues, these can be fixed. But if you can't get or keep customers, arguably you don't have a business at all.

Now, I believe hotels are different in this matter both in the way they get customers (on the whole) and indeed, importantly, in the things they do to keep customers.

I cannot think of many other business types that are so utterly dependent on third parties for business. Certainly not in a B2C (business to consumer) capacity anyway. You see, I could open the doors of a hotel tomorrow, stick every room on Booking.com and other similar OTAs (online travel agents) and sooner or later I'd get customers. The downside of course is that I'd have to pay somewhere between 15-20% of my margin for each customer. Of course if the normal OTAs aren't performing, I could pop over to a daily deal site like Groupon or TravelZoo and give a great value offer in exchange for a huge chunk of margin PLUS a commission percentage the wrong side of 20% or even 30%! The fact of the matter is this: getting some customers when you open a hotel is relatively easy if you use these tools ready-made to shovel customers into your bedrooms. So easy in fact, that hotels have become lazy to the point where few of the thousands of hoteliers I've met in my career know anything about marketing their hotel to get customers outside of these expensive resources.

Now, this brings me to this notion of keeping customers. Most sophisticated businesses have a plan to get you back to spend more, and they'll do various things to keep you as a customer. Some coffee shops use loyalty cards; car mechanics remind you when you're due for a service; if you buy a book on Amazon.com you'll be certain to receive a "you might also like these" email. Yet I sit, writing this book with over 8 years in hotel marketing, having stayed in hundreds of hotels in the past couple of years alone and I can honestly count on one hand those that had a strategic plan to keep me as a customer.

My issue, and the reason I wrote this book is simply this: the marketing ideas, views and practices in our industry are falling behind and leaving huge numbers of hotels struggling to make a profit while the third parties are getting richer. And importantly – it doesn't have to be like this!

The premise of this book frankly couldn't be simpler. If as a hotelier, you would like to make more profit, this book will share proven practices, ideas and marketing techniques to drive more new and repeat bookings to come to you direct, without commission.

If that hotelier is you—then read on dear friend. I hope to open your eyes to new and exciting ways of doing business, the likes of which you may never have heard before, but I promise you that everything written within in these pages has already been tried and tested in my own hotel, and many others.

Equally, there will undoubtedly be elements within this book that you currently use to market your business—in these instances I would implore you to make tweaks or leaps in your approach. Marketing in its truest form is about marginal gains to achieve a better-desired result.

I wish you the best of luck in attracting lots of new and repeat customers and I salute your attempts. Now, let's make you a great deal more money.

HOW TO USE THIS BOOK

Every customer has the potential to be a customer for life. It is worthwhile to remind yourself and your staff of that every day. The reality is that if you:

a) Deliver a WOW experience
b) Market to them effectively

...Then there's really no reason why they shouldn't come back.

This book is written from the ideological standpoint that you as the owner or marketer of this business have an obligation to maximise the business from each and every single person that comes into contact with your hotel.

Prospective Customers should be marketed to until they buy or tell you they're not interested.

Customers should be thanked for their custom and encouraged and incentivised to come back and encouraged and incentivised to refer custom to you.

Loyal Customers should be shown great thanks and gratitude for their repeated custom and should be repeatedly encouraged and incentivised to return and refer business.

Former Customers should be told in no uncertain terms that you miss their custom and should be encouraged and incentivised to return.

These areas will be discussed more in the Database Segmentation chapter, but mentioning them here is important because as a marketer of a business these four instructions are your responsibility. Get these four things right, and you will successfully get and keep customers.

PART ONE of this book is a list of marketing tools and techniques we use in my business, both to market The Cranleigh Boutique but also to market the hotels we manage in our marketing agency Wow Guest Hotel Marketing. This section of the book provides an overview of the elements that make up the marketing toolbox.

PART TWO is a section of the book dedicated to exclusively to email marketing. Emails continue to be the one form of marketing the drives more direct zero commission business than any other form of marketing for the hotels we work with.

PART THREE brings it all together. This section explains how to implement the complete marketing system for your business, working autonomously to target your ideal customers. This as taken me literally years to develop, and is one of the most influential factors in the ability to reduce dependency on the OTAs. To understand it fully, it is strongly recommended that you read and understand all the elements in PART ONE first.

So in short, read this book chronologically. Don't skip over sections in PART ONE because you're already using that particular piece of marketing to good effect. Instead read on; the likelihood is that you'll find a slightly different way of using that particular marketing tool that could result in even better results.

More information about each marketing tool and technique is provided on www.moredirectbookings.com/resources

Visit this page to access more in-depth explanations, practical examples, step-by-step video tutorials and handy diagrams to aid your understanding and implementation of each marketing tool.

HOW NOT TO USE THIS BOOK

This book is not for brand marketers. This book is for hoteliers who want more sales. As such, this book is best suited to independent properties or small groups of hotels. What I mean by the above statement is that there are two types of marketing:

a) Direct Response Marketing
b) Brand Marketing

Direct Response Marketing, as the name suggests, is about encouraging action from the recipient. The clear objective of any piece of Direct Response Marketing is to get leads or get sales. If an email, or a direct mailing or a Facebook campaign results in sales, it's deemed successful because of the volume of sales and the amount of revenue that was created as a direct result.

Brand Marketing is actually what most "marketing people" do. The objective of brand marketing is to create materials, campaigns and online activity that reflect the business in a favourable manner that may result in a sale somewhere down the line.

I do not wish to discredit Brand Marketing—it has an essential part to play in the hotel marketing mix. Great photography, for example, is a brand marketing cost that should be invested. But this book focuses on the stuff that brings in the cash.

Very often the size and price point of your hotel will dictate whether you should be using direct response or brand marketing. The Savoy's royal suite at £15,000 per night, for example, is unlikely to use direct response marketing. If the marketing team there were going to do anything, it would use brand-marketing techniques to market this particular product. On the other side of the scale, a B&B priced at £50 per night that places a full-page ad in a newspaper just promoting nice imagery and a nice logo without a meaningful call to action or offer to encourage the sale, would be, I suspect a poor use of marketing budget. Premium alcohol spirits, perfumes and watches use brand marketing—spending millions to reinforce the ideals of the brand message. Chances are if you are reading this book, your marketing budget must deliver tangible results that you can quantify. If this is the case, this book will teach you ways to maximise your marketing budget into heads in beds.

WHY ONLY *READING* THIS BOOK IS A WASTE OF TIME.

Picking this book up and nodding all the way through, then getting busy and popping it back on the shelf thinking that was really useful—will not drive your business forward. Forgive me for stating the obvious, but this book will only impact your business if you put these proven tools and systems into ACTION. Or, if you don't physically have enough time in the day, get someone to take action for you.

Action is key, but so is mindset. Getting and keeping customers should be the number one priority in your hotel. Remember that any problem in the business is never as bad when you have a healthy batch of new and repeat customers coming through your doors on a regular basis.

Now with these "housekeeping rules" out of the way, let's get started to help you get and keep customers more affordably, effectively and regularly. Let's get started.

PART ONE

TRACKING TELEPHONE NUMBERS

The chapter of Tracking Telephone Numbers has purposefully been placed as the first marketing tool because it is an absolute MUST for each and every hotel. Most hoteliers don't know what makes their phone ring. Tracking numbers typically costs £1 per month and allows you to assess what marketing is working and what isn't.

In brief, a tracking telephone number is a separate local or national number that instantly redirects to the desired call destination--typically reception--but allows you to assess where the call has come from. So if you run five local print ads in five local newspapers and use a tracking number for each, at the end of the duration of those ads you could quickly and efficiently ascertain which ad performed the best. Importantly in month two, the sensible thing to do would be to invest a bigger chunk of your marketing budget on the ads that worked really well, and scrap the ones that didn't work. This marketing tool is particularly effective in offline marketing where you are limited by the amount of tracking you can do, but we also use it extensively online too because some customers still like to speak to a person rather than go online to book.

An unsung benefit of tracking numbers is that it allows you to track and measure how many calls are being missed. Having spent my entire career (almost) calling hotels, it is worrying just how many calls to reception go unanswered. As a hotel, there are only so many ways that customers can buy from you, and if you are missing calls, you're missing sales. I'll discuss how this can be avoided in later chapters, but for the purpose of tracking telephone numbers, if you have never used them, this would be an ideal opportunity to ascertain how many calls are being missed. Some months before writing this chapter we ran a test with a new client we had taken on in England. We simply changed the telephone number on the website to a tracking number and in 8 weeks, a whopping 608 calls were going unanswered! What was clear is that this hotel required an overflow call answering service to manage the sheer volume of calls that were going unanswered. Within a few days we plugged a big hole in their business that cost less than a coffee from Starbucks.

An additional feature of a telephone tracking number is something known as a "Call Whisper"—typically your investment is an extra £1 per month and the premise is that moments before the caller is connected, a whisper comes down the phone explaining where the call has come from. So, for example, if you are looking for a general overview when answering the phone, if you pick up the line, you can set the call to whisper things like "Website", "Facebook" or "TripAdvisor" to give you or your staff a real time idea of what is working. All the important statistics would still be available to you by exporting a report, but this would be a useful insight if, for example, you have just posted a new offer on your Facebook page with a telephone call to action; you could assess how immediate the response was. In short, it's a very affordable way of assessing quickly and efficiently what's making your telephone ring.

The company we use at Wow Guest Hotel Marketing is one of the biggest in the UK—Invoco. They charge £1 +VAT per tracking telephone number, £1 + VAT per call whisper and mere pennies for each call. It barely registers on our outgoings. Additionally, everything can be set up online. I have sat in front of clients with a laptop; purchased a tracking telephone number, redirected it to their reception and called the number in the space of about 2 minutes, often to their complete astonishment.

For a full list of tracking telephone number companies and other suppliers we use referenced throughout this book, visit www.moredirectbookings.com/resources

GOOGLE ANALYTICS

No website should be without Google Analytics. It's a free, cloud-based (i.e. no installation required) service that allows you to track and measure where your website traffic is coming from. There's much more you can use it for including things like measuring results on advertising platforms like Google AdWords, understanding how users actually navigate through your website, where they tend to leave the website, etc. If you're new to it, don't get yourself bogged down with all the bells and whistles; the fundamental purpose should be to help you save money you're probably wasting, and help you spend more money in places which are tending to perform well.

Basic Google Analytics Uses:

1) Traffic Sources

This refers to understanding where your website visitors are actually coming from to get to your website. I'd expect for a typical hotel, the top 10 traffic sources will include search engines, OTAs, meta search sites like Trivago and perhaps some hotel organisations like Best Loved that you might be a part of.

The key here is to look for local tourism websites that seem to be delivering traffic to you—perhaps those that you wouldn't necessarily expect to be in the top 10 or 20 and certainly sites where you would not ordinarily advertise. These small websites that are already bringing you traffic may just be the best use of your marketing budget. To give you an example of what I'm referring to, a client of ours; a country house hotel in Scotland, actively promotes their "pet-friendly" selling point. As such, when we took a good look into their analytics, we found that a small website dedicated to showcasing the best pet-friendly hotels in Scotland was delivering a strong amount of traffic in comparison to the likes of Booking.com. We approached this website and took out one of their "sponsored" advertising spots for £50 for the year! Almost over night the already strong numbers doubled with this additional exposure on this tiny website.

Now, this one piece of marketing insight isn't going to pack out the hotel every night for the next 10 years, but this is a brilliant example of marginal gains to improve occupancy. For about the same commission of one booking from Booking.com, we were able to increase the number of visitors to their website. My advice to you is to study your Google Analytics carefully, think about your key selling points and find websites that are bringing you organic traffic—then approach them and enquire about advertising space. Fish where the fish are—if it's working, amplify it for more success.

> A detailed step-by-step video on how to get analytics set up and what to look for is available to view on www.moredirectbookings.com/resources

2) Bounce Rates

The bounce rate is an important consideration. A "bounce" is a website visitor that leaves your website without doing anything or clicking any link, thus "bouncing" straight off it. A bounce suggests that your website was not relevant or was not what the user was looking for. With this in mind, be wary of websites that deliver you traffic with high bounce rates—anything over 40% is high. A typical example is language that suggests the product is better than it actually is. A prospective customer might read all about the "boutique" nature of a "luxury" hotel, when in truth the user sees poor quality imagery and "B&B" featured everywhere. Bouncing is all about relevance. The more you can match your website copy and imagery to that of your text ads, image ads, and descriptions on other sites, the lower your bounce rate will be. An area where bounce rates are of particular importance is when you're using pay-per-click advertising—for obvious reasons if you are spending £2 per click and they leave the website within 5 seconds, it's a quick way to waste money.

3) Dwell Time and Flow

The dwell time is simply the amount of time a website visitor remains on the website. The flow shows you how users are using your site and importantly where most people are leaving. You might find that an uncommon amount of visitors are leaving your website on the gallery page—this might be because the images take far too long to load and therefore your website visitors get bored and leave. It might sound a little fickle, but this is exactly the type of thing that impacts sales to your hotel. Similarly, many hotel websites that we've worked on over the years have very high bounce rates on the "book online" page, typically because the reservation tool is far too slow to load or is too confusing.

Summary

If you're starting out with Google Analytics, don't get too technical—there's an ocean of data ready and waiting to be explored, but for the non-tech-savvy newbie, it can prove overwhelming. Start by once a week making an appointment with yourself to check in and see which websites have brought you the most traffic and look for opportunities to increase those numbers. It's often said the devil is in the detail—well I personally believe that in marketing, the money is in the data. Find data trends, make small, shrewd investments and you'll be able to capitalise.

Last point on this chapter—if you're struggling to get this set up, don't do it yourself! Go on Fiverr.com and find a recommended person to do it for you for $5 USD. That's approximately £3.50 or €4. If you're not used to doing these things, you can spend several hours trying to figure it out yourself or spend 5 minutes and $5 and have it done for you, normally within 48 hours. That's a much smarter use of your time and money, wouldn't you say?

For video tutorials on how to make full use of Google Analytics, visit www.moredirectbookings.com/resources

LEAD MAGNETS

A lead magnet or "lead bait" is a way of encouraging sign-ups, so that you can capture prospective customers' information and start to build a relationship and encourage the prospective customer to buy.

Much the same as a "subscribe to our newsletter" request, you give the website visitor the opportunity to give you their information like email address and first name, but you incentivise them to do this by giving away value. This value might be in the shape of a discount, special offers or my particular favourite—useful information that helps the prospective customer to make the right booking decision. Ultimately, when you think about it, for most leisure guests, they likely know very little about your hotel, the area or what one can see and do when they stay with you. The smart thing to do here is to actually do the work for the customer by compiling a list of the best things to see and do, as well as all the local secrets that rarely attract tourists. We call these *Lead Magnet Guides* and examples of successful guides include things like *Our Favourite Walking Routes, The Insiders Guide to [Town],* and *The [Town] Family Fun Guide*. The very essence here is that:

    a) You are encouraging the prospective customer to give you their data email address and name
    b) You are making the buying decision easier for the prospective customer

Now, hopefully you can see how much more effective this will be than what every other hotel does—request that customers subscribe to their newsletter. If you take nothing else of relevance from this book DO NOT FORGET THIS ONE KEY STATEMENT—subscribe to our newsletter is dead.

In the early 2000s, everyone raved about this wonderful new medium known as *email*. Oh the enjoyment we all revelled in sending and receiving emails. How exciting it was to receive newsletters from our favourite companies. As I write this in 2015, I don't know many people who receive fewer than 100 emails per day in their work account. In short—it is no longer exciting to receive a newsletter from a company, no matter how nice the hotel looks from all the wonderful imagery you've carefully displayed on your site. Frankly, it's dull, lazy marketing to assume prospective customers are so incredibly interested in you that they will part with their valuable information in exchange for a newsletter. Times have changed and if you want to maximise the sale from your website, you need a lead magnet, not a link to subscribe to a newsletter.

These lead magnet guides are also very useful and effective at building trust. The information you are imparting helps to position your hotel as a trusted advisor. You are not some sleazy salesman saying please book my hotel; you are there to carefully advise the prospective customer to help them make the right decision.

To understand why these lead magnet guides work, you must understand and acknowledge that the booking decision process has changed dramatically in the last 10 years or so. No longer do prospective customers find a hotel and book. They hop around a dozen sites before finding half a dozen hotels that look nice and study them in intricate detail before eventually coming to an emotional conclusion backed up by logic that THIS hotel is the right one for them. Sure this is a sweeping generalisation, but the premise is true because customers have far more choice than they used to have. Understanding that the journey to the "book now" button is a long and complex one is fundamental to the impact on your hotel.

If you can stay present and front of mind during this booking decision process—which may take weeks or even months—then your chances of securing the business increases dramatically. Moreover, your chances of securing a direct booking is far more likely if you can give away a lead magnet guide in exchange for the prospective customer's valuable contact information, and then follow up with some relationship-building email correspondence that is engaging and encourages the sale. Email auto-responders are the way forward here and I discuss these in the next chapter.

> For actual examples of lead-magnets that are working right now to drive business to some of the hotels we work with, and some inspiration as to what your hotel can use to incentive website visitors to share their contact information with you, visit www.moredirectbookings.com/resources

EMAIL AUTO-RESPONDERS

This section on email auto-responders explains the following:
- How to automate emails to your subscribers
- How to ensure you avoid bombardment
- Why email auto-responders work

Email-auto responders are a superb way to stay in touch with a subscriber after they have shown interest in the hotel. As the name suggests, they are automated, so once you have the system set up, it works like clockwork. They are nothing more than a series of emails that are scheduled to be delivered on set days after a certain action has been taken. So consider as an example that you send a monthly email out on the 28th day of each month to your database. After a quick search on Google I have ended up on your hotel's website on the 1st of the month. After about 10 minutes of looking around the website, I am interested in booking your hotel, but not today, so rather than book, I decide to subscribe to your newsletter or download your lead magnet and leave the website. I hear nothing for 27 days until a generic email comes on the 28th of that month—by which time I've forgotten all about your hotel and booked somewhere else.

This is commonplace with hotels—lack of meaningful follow-up that allows a warm prospective customer who is interested in booking your hotel to go cold, undervalued and take their purchase to a competitor. This is why a set of auto-responding emails can be so powerful in keeping in touch, sharing some information, building the relationship with the prospective customer and encouraging them to make the leap from being a contemplator to a booker. But, I hasten to add, simply emailing them automatically won't do the job, you need to adopt a carefully thought-out methodical approach to close the sale.

After rigorous testing over many years, we have crafted a winning formula that works like this:

Email 1 – Day 0 – Thank you for downloading
Email 2 – Day 1 – Did you know?
Email 3 – Day 4 – Recent 'Excellent' TripAdvisor Review
Email 4 – Day 9 – Why I love what I do
Email 5 – Day 15 – Staff member highlight
Email 6 – Day 20 – Get off the fence
Email 7 – Day 22 – Get off the fence follow up

Email 1
Include a few short words to thank them for subscribing to your newsletter or downloading your lead magnet. Explain in this email that from time to time you'll send them info that you think would interest them about the hotel such as news and offers.

Email 2
Follow up the next day, thanking them again for subscribing or downloading. Then, share a short, interesting fact about the hotel. It might be that you have a 96% review score, or that 3 out of 5 guests that visited last year have made bookings again for this year. Some statistic or fact that illustrates that your hotel is great at what it does.

Email 3
Take a screen shot of a 5 star review from TripAdvisor and include it in the email. Ideally choose a person with a clear view of themselves in their thumbnail picture to make it seem as tangible and as real as possible.

Email 4
Write 150 words explaining why you love running this hotel. This notion seems foreign amongst hoteliers in my experience but it's powerful. Every customer wants to buy from the enthusiastic hotelier who loves what they do and is prepared to go that extra mile—get this across in no more than 150 words

and it will set you head and shoulders above the competition.

Email 5
Highlight, with a picture, a staff member who's great at their job. It might be the head chef, the cleaning maid who's been with the company over 10 years; it might be a hotel dog if you have one to promote your pet-friendly benefit. Make the staff as real and as personable as possible.

Email 6
Up to this point you've not overtly tried to sell to them at all. Now's the time to get them off the fence and to move them from being a contemplator to being a customer. Explain that as far as you're aware they've not booked yet and you'd like to change that, then give them a time-sensitive offer to book with a clear call to action.

Email 7
Follow up on that get-off-the-fence offer you sent them a few days earlier, again reiterating the deadline and the specific action you want them to take.

Now, most commonly the response to my suggestion of sending seven emails in a little more than three weeks is one of fear. I continue to find it utterly fascinating that hotel owners or managers would rather risk the prospective customer going somewhere else than do everything within their power to secure the sale for fear of slightly annoying them with too many emails. It's completely bonkers! Having said that; if you sent them an email every day for 3 weeks that simply said
- "buy now"
- "please buy now"
- "why haven't you bought, you really should buy now"

...then obviously this would be annoying.

But using this proven method of ours, you are merely providing the customer with enough information and enough gentle follow-ups to be front of mind when they come to making an informed decision.

Moreover, these people are not your customers! They've not bought anything from you at this stage, so you lose nothing by adopting this approach.

What's more is that setting up a sequence of auto-responding emails is really quite easy. The system I personally use in my business and for all my clients is Active Camapign. With no prior experience of using auto-responding emails, you can have these live very swiftly and there's every chance your competitors won't be using them so you'll have a distinct advantage.

> To download a complete "done-for-you" template for my entire email auto-responding system, visit www.moredirectbookings.com/resources

CUSTOMER RELATIONSHIP MANAGEMENT (CRM) SYSTEM

Without question, every hotel should use a Customer Relationship Management system (CRM). Simply put a CRM is a programme that allows you to segment your database and communicate with them, typically via email. Chances are your property management or reservation system will have one integrated into it, but chances are it won't be great, which is why we always recommend specialist programmes.

Now the key difference between a CRM and a simple email broadcast system is, frankly, how you use it. And in many respects it's a mindset issue. In an earlier chapter I discussed the way in which most hotels view their customers—get them in, hope they come back. In truth very few hotels actively work to strengthen the relationship they have with their customers. Instead, they rely on a sales message every month to entice them back, with little or no thought to the context of the customer. For example, a customer who checked out yesterday, may today be sent an email with a great value offer. This would happen because there is a lack of segmentation and process. A much better email to send would be "thank you for your custom"—a CRM system will help you to systemise this type of thing so that your communication serves to strengthen the relationship with your customers, not weaken it.

A good CRM system will, of course, allow you to measure the level of engagement of each of your customers, and provide plenty of automatic features so you can communicate with your customers autonomously; normally when they take an action like submitting their details to download the lead magnet.

Simply put, a good CRM, used effectively, will allow you to build and nurture the relationship with your customers so they spend more with you.

There are plenty of cheap and cheerful email providers. The likes of Mail Chimp, Get Response, Constant Contact and a seemingly endless list of programmes allow you to build emails using an easy-to-use drag and drop process to create attractive emails that can be sent in bulk. I'm not against these programmes; I've personally used most of them across various businesses I've run and indeed for some of the hotels we serve at Wow Guest Hotel Marketing. But when it comes to CRM systems, there's only one I use and recommend, Active Campaign.

Having used, tried and frankly been frustrated by so many, I stumbled across Active Camapign which does everything a marketer needs to effectively manage the relationship with customers and increase sales. Rather than go on an Active Campaign loving crusade listing all its benefits and features, this book is not intended to sell you a CRM, only to demonstrate why and how a good CRM system can benefit your sales.

> For more information on why I use Active Campaign in my own business and how I make use of all its features to drive new customers to our hotel clients, visit www.moredirectbookings.com/resources

LEAD SCORING

One of the reasons why I personally use and recommend Active Campaign is for its Lead Scoring feature. Lead Scoring is simply a way of measuring engagement. The most engaged customers are the ones that interact with your content the most (be it email, website, videos, etc.). These typically will be the ones most likely to book, but (and it's a big BUT) offer no guarantee that they will book. It's good business sense to identify those customers who are showing willingness to book a stay but for whatever reason have not crossed over the line yet—and be proactive in getting them over the fence. Lead Scoring is the best way to do this.

Each interaction is measured with a score. A typical lead scoring system might look like this:

Open email – 1 point
Click link within email – 3 points
Share email with a friend – 5 points
Visit a page on your website – 1 point
Visit the booking page on website – 5 points
Watch a video on your website – 3 points

On their own this point system might seem a little meaningless, but over time, the accrual of points can be extremely helpful in understanding your customers. Here are a few examples:

Example 1

Let's say you've been sending monthly emails for the last year with a reasonable amount of success, but you think they should be performing better. You might choose the top 100 most engaged customers on your database i.e. the 100 email records with the highest lead score over the designated period of time. You send each of these customers a special email requesting feedback on the last few emails. You might even go so far as to acknowledge that these customers are the most engaged; "that as a valued customer who actively engages with our content, we'd really appreciate your feedback"—this will show the customer that they're not just another email address on your list, serving to strengthen the relationship you have with these particular customers.

Example 2

Lead Scoring on Active Campaign also allows you to automatically communicate with customers who are showing high levels of engagements in a short period of time. One customer may for example:

- Open an email = 1 point
- Click an email = 3 points
- Visit 6 pages of the website = 1 point x 6 = 6 points

TOTAL = 10 points

Now you might set up a rule stating that if a member of your database accrues 10 points or more in a single 24-hour period, then an email will be sent to them from the General Manager stating something like this:

Dear [firstname]

John here from X hotel, I trust all's well.

I noticed just now that you've been having a good look around our website and wondered if I can help with anything?

If the hotel stay you're thinking of booking is for you, what sort of time are you looking to visit? Let me know and I'll see what I can do to secure you a free upgrade provided we have the availability.

Thanks for being a customer of X hotel.

*Kindest regards,
John Smith
General Manager*

An email like this will set you miles ahead of the competition in securing this customer's business. And the best part of it all—you had this whole process automated.

Example 3

Lead Scoring isn't only relevant to email marketing, you will also be able to track customers who visit your website out of the blue. Let's say a customer lands on your website from Google or an OTA or TripAdvisor, provided they are in the same location as the CRM has registered on the system (known as an IP address) the system will register that "Gary Philips" is visiting the website, for example. And, as above, if Gary hits a lead score of 10 points or more, within a 24-hour period, you can automate the same email to him.

What this means is that you will have the ability to see who is showing genuine interest in booking your hotel long before they make an enquiry or call to book.

It's absolutely revolutionary in its ability to engage with people who might buy but without a little nudge, probably won't.

To clarify then, most CRMs in my experience don't have lead scoring set up within it; you have to purchase additional software or plugins, which is another reason why I fully endorse Active Campaign as a CRM.

To see actual working examples of lead scoring in action, visit www.moredirectbookings.com/resources

PRINTED NEWSLETTER

Now if you've seen the word "printed" and can't get past the fact that this already sounds expensive, you may well be pleasantly surprised. Print and postage doesn't have to be expensive IF you find the right supplier, and the message goes out to the right people.

A printed newsletter is frankly the best tool there is to build and maintain relationships with your customers. And if I've not made this point crystal clear already, the most important, fundamental underlining principle of this book is to equip you with the tools to help you build, maintain and strengthen the relationships with your customers and prospective customers. The reason for this hopefully should be obvious, but for clarity's sake, let's imagine that you run a 20-bedroom hotel and you have a database of 50,000 engaged customers and prospects who enjoy reading your emails, looking at your images, watching your videos and ultimately they find themselves talking about you regularly.

As a 20-bedroom property open all year round, you have 7,300 room nights to sell. Now, let's imagine of those 50,000 contacts, 0.5% (which is a low conversion rate by the way) of them book two-night stays every time you send an email.

50,000 people x 0.5% conversion x 2 room nights = 500 room nights sold per email.

So that's 6,000 room nights sold each year for each email you send based on one per month—giving you an occupancy of 83% just from email marketing – which is completely devoid of commission by the way!

Now, what does this all have to do with printed newsletters, you might be wondering? Well a great deal actually. You see, to be able to get yourself into a position whereby your email marketing is consistently pulling in four- and five-figure revenues from customers eager to visit you again and again, you need STRONG RELATIONSHIPS with your customers and a printed newsletter every few months sent out to your customers will help in building those relationships so that your other marketing channels (namely email marketing from the example above) will work more effectively. To put it another way, if you buy cold email data and send out an offer, you can expect a very poor response, let alone all sorts of spam complaints and potential legal issues. To refrain therefore from labouring the point—an engaged database will be a responsive one.

Ok, so printed newsletters can be good at building relationships--but what goes in them and what do they look like? Well, a good printed newsletter will combine a healthy dose of hotel news, entertaining snippets of information, "non-relevant" content and a good amount of informal chat. This printed newsletter serves as a conversation between you--the hotel manager, marketer or otherwise--and the customer. Important point here being that it comes from a real, living, breathing person. Someone with a pulse must send this. Hotels are buildings and do not send correspondence to customers! (Most) people do not build relationships with inanimate objects like buildings; they develop relationships with people and the chances are (depending upon the size of your property) most customers have zero interaction with the General Manager, the owner or some other top figure within the hotel responsible for most of the experiences the customer felt during their stay. In short, as the big wig in your hotel, this is your opportunity to have a good old chit chat and chin wag with your customers!

Before I move on to discuss the specific content of one of these printed newsletters, if you're still sceptical about this notion, consider this for a few moments . . . newspapers and magazines are what your customers read to relax and unwind and inform themselves about things they wish to be informed about. In other words, of all the ways in which your customers read stuff, newspapers and magazines are the preferred medium. With this in mind you might safely assume that it would be a wise thing to put the stuff you want your customers to know that will favourably encourage present and future hotel booking decisions into the preferred medium and style of the customer.

Now, in terms of the content—it doesn't have to be an 80-page glossy magazine. Far from it. Some of the best newsletters I receive from all sorts of companies are 4 pages (that's effectively one side of A3 paper front and back). It also doesn't necessarily have to be in colour. In many instances, a black and white newsletter can serve to stand out much better than full colour, not to mention the cost differences here.

Front page—manager's note to the customer. A 400- to 500-word personal letter from you to the customer covering anything from information about staff members, the new goose feather pillows you've just placed in every room, the big event soon to launch in your locality, etc. Think of it like a post card—a few hundred words on what's new and, indirectly, what the customer is missing by not visiting soon. This "letter" should include a pen-scribbled signature and should be specifically from the hotel owner or manager. Plus it absolutely must have a picture of this owner or manager somewhere in full view. Remember this newsletter is about building a relationship between you and the customer, so make yourself as real as possible.

Other than the front page welcome letter, fill out the content with features like:
- Employee of the month
- Customer of the month
- Calendar of what to do in your area

- Mini interview with a member of staff
- Specials on the menu this month
- Reasons to visit this month
- Recent excellent reviews from TripAdvisor
- Quiz questions
- Something silly and completely unrelated to make the customer laugh or smile

Make sure you place lots of images throughout; keep it engaging and entertaining. Now, when it comes to pricing this perceptively expensive medium to engage with your customers, it's likely cheaper than you might believe. The Wow Guest Hotel Marketing printed newsletter has been printed by the same supplier for the last few years and they recently quoted us for 2,000 at 12 pence each. That's £240 for 2,000 newsletters. Once we'd thrown in postage, we were looking at just shy of £1 to print, pack and send to each customer. So what we tend to do with most of our hotel clients is to only send to the top 25% of our customers and have a stash of newsletters to hand out upon departure from the hotel. At 12 pence per newsletter it is very cost effective way to engage with customers.

There will be, I suspect, a desire to throw in an offer or a sales message with a clear call to action. This is a mistake. Your printed newsletter is there to build and nurture the relationship with your customer—not to sell to them. The credibility of this new mini publication will be jeopardised should you splash a sales offer all over it.

For examples and content ideas of a printed newsletter, plus how to discern which customers should be sent one and which customers really shouldn't, visit
www.moredirectbookings.com/resources

FACEBOOK ADVERTISING

At the time of writing this (early 2015) Facebook Ads are the most exciting, cheapest form of online advertising available to businesses. Things change significantly and quickly in the world of digital marketing, so how long this chapter will be accurate is unknown, so don't delay! The reason I and many other professional marketers are so excited about Facebook ads is that we can buy super targeted traffic for mere pennies, and they are significantly cheaper than most other advertising tools.

The best example I always use is weddings. Let's say you have £1,000 to spend on wedding marketing and are toying with the idea of running a press ad in a national wedding publication, which will probably be no more than a quarter page. You are also considering advertising in a local generic magazine which might buy you a full page. Now, if you consider the advantages of these two, you might come to the conclusion that the national publication will give you presence to millions of brides-to-be and the local publication will give you presence to fewer brides-to-be but a bit more targeted in terms of location. Disadvantages are that in the national you're competing with dozens of other venues and effectively advertising to people hundreds of miles away who might render your advertisement irrelevant by your location. And in the local publication, much of your money is being wasted on people who are not even getting married!

Now let's say you took that £1,000 to Facebook advertising. Well you might want to target women between the ages of 20-40 within a 50-mile radius of the hotel who have a relationship status of "engaged." And you'd want to get those ads running on a pay-per-click basis, so that you only actually pay when someone clicks on the ad, irrespective of how many people see those ads. Lastly, you'd want to target those clicks toward a page where the interested bride-to-be would be able to learn more information about your wedding facilities and make an enquiry so you can capture information.

If all that sounds great, you'll be even more impressed to learn that in a recent wedding push for a client in the UK (January 2015) we created a wedding Facebook advertising campaign that delivered clicks at approximately £0.18 per click and £1.06 per enquiry. To date approximately 1 in 5 for of those enquiries have converted into a sale in excess of £3,000. So in real terms for every £5.30 we spend on Facebook, we made over £3,000 for the client.

There are multiple ways to use advertising on Facebook by choosing the specific objective you want—impressions, clicks, post engagement, offer retrieval, etc. Explanation of each of these elements would require a book in itself, and much more information on the subject can be found on
www.moredirectbookings.com/resources

Suffice it to say that Facebook advertising is without question, the most exciting and cost-effective way of targeting your ideal customer, and provided it is used with some effective marketing systems, you'll find it an incredible asset to driving your hotel business forward.

GOOGLE ADWORDS

It would be well worth taking note that the largest OTA in the world--Booking.com--is one of Google Adwords' biggest customers. That in itself should spark your interest and suggest that this is an advertising medium worthy of your attention and respect. The challenge with Google Adwords is that whilst it may be relatively straightforward to set up and get going with some ads, mastering this medium takes practice, patience and money. Which is why it's no surprise that of all the hoteliers I know, approximately 4 in 5 have tried Google Adwords at some point but have given up on it because they lost a lot of money very quickly. The reason this happens a great deal is that without a full understanding of how to minimise cost-per-click whilst maximising click-throughs within the settings of Adwords, you run the risk of spending a lot of clicks (and therefore money) on irrelevant traffic that has no intention of ever buying from you.

Similarly, ensuring that the process is relevant throughout for the user is essential. Spending £1 to get a prospective customer to your website with the enticement of a spring offer, only to then send them to a hotel's homepage where they have to search quite intently to find that spring offer distorts the flow for the user and in many cases can leave the user feeling frustrated and they leave the website. Relevance and a clear path are essential when spending money on online advertising especially when it's Google Adwords given that the cost–per-click can be expensive.

In comparison to Facebook Advertising, the cost-per-click is significantly higher on Adwords. To appear in the top 3 ads for "Hotels in London" for example would set you back (at the time of writing this in early 2015) anywhere between £2-7 per click! It's highly competitive. Facebook allows you to target people with the intent to travel to London for less than £1 per click. So why would you ever want to spend money on Google Adwords when there are other, more targeted, cheaper advertising platforms to generate traffic to your site? Well, because the reality is, that's where most people start their buying process. Being at the front of the queue when someone searches "hotels in [your town] for this weekend" has its obvious benefits. Facebook ads comparatively have you essentially turning up and hoping for the best. Adwords allows you to be in the right place when people are taking action to buy.

Similarly to Facebook ads, this topic requires an entire book to fully explain what you should and shouldn't do with Adwords, but in almost every case, there is a very strong argument for each hotel to be using them in some capacity, and provided you know your cost per sale from the average OTA booking (see chapter on Measuring CPL and CPS), you can reasonably and accurately assess how much better off you are by spending your money with Google than an OTA through commission.

Much more detail about how to set up ads, back-end lead-capture and how to ensure that wastage is kept to a minimum can be found at www.moredirectbookings.com/resources

MEASURING COST-PER-LEAD (CPL) AND COST-PER-SALE (CPS)

There's a popular phrase that says, "what gets measured, gets managed." I'm acutely aware that to the unseasoned hotel marketer reading this book, that all these statistics and metrics about open rates, click-through rates, cost-per-click and other such jargon might all seem lovely and good to know, but they might perceptively carry little meaning. And let's face it, the biggest thing you want to know is whether the money you're spending on marketing is actually resulting in actual sales. And crucially, how much are you spending to get the sale? Because if you're spending £50 to get a customer that delivers only £40 profit, you've got a problem.

So with that in mind, ignore all the other nonsense metrics and focus your time and effort into knowing the only 2 that really matter.

Cost-per-lead and Cost-per-sale.

That is, the money you spent in acquiring the prospective customer's information so that you can continue to market to them to encourage the sale.

And, the money you spent in acquiring the sale.

Armed with these two statistics after delivery of a marketing campaign, you'll know, with a high degree of accuracy, how much it costs you to drive the business forward. Equally, if your average booking delivers £200, then by using an OTA at 15% commission you know that your cost per sale is £30. Comparatively, after some testing, it would not be uncommon for you to consistently derive 3 new bookings from £30 from online advertising, giving you a cost per sale of £10—in real terms that would mean OTAs deliver you £200 revenue for £30, and direct marketing systems using online advertising deliver you £600 for £30 – a 200% better return on your marketing investment! Hence, this is the reason why those hotels who embrace these marketing techniques that we encourage and have perfected over the years command significantly more profit than those hotels who simply rely on third parties to keep their business afloat.

Equally cost-per-lead is important. Driving customers to a specific landing page where the page is designed to encourage customers to download a lead magnet or indeed simply subscribe to a newsletter might, for example, convert website visitors to newsletter subscribers at a cost of £1—so your cost-per-lead is £1. You might then send them through a 3-week email auto-responding campaign at which 1 in 10 convert to a sale. So in this case, here are your measurements:

Cost-per-lead = £1
Cost-per-sale = £10

The lead time on these statistics might be 3-4 weeks as you're not asking for the sale outright, but once you have tested these statistics, you have the necessary marketing systems in place to convert these prospective customers into paying customers; you are well on your way to becoming free from ever again needing to pay commission for bookings.

Using the above numbers as an example, you are paying £10 to acquire one customer yourself through automated marketing systems and are paying £30 to acquire one customer via an OTA.

The same process applies to other routes to market besides online advertising. For example, if you send a direct marketing piece to a segment of existing customers in the post, and it costs

£2,500 to print and send, and delivers 200 bookings, you have achieved a cost per sale of £12.50. Not a bad return compared to the OTA example previously of £30 per sale. Armed with this knowledge that this mailing piece can achieve a cost-per-sale of £12.50, you might decide to deliver to the rest of your database, knowing full well that even if the next batch underperforms and delivers only £25 cost per sale, that's still better than relying on the OTAs!

Continuing with the example of the average booking rate of £200 and a low level of commission of 15%, let's say if you start using the daily deal websites to drive business which commonly requires 22% commission, your cost-per-sale for these websites is £44! The question you should be asking yourself before using these types of agents is if I had £44 to spend on marketing, how would I do it? Facebook ads, Google Ads, postcards for repeat custom, postcards for referral custom, newsletters sent in the post, a £44 bar tab as an enticement sent via email?

My point here is that once you know how much your cost-per-sale figure is for each marketing method, you will start to be able to measure profitability success rates accurately and steer your marketing money and resources toward the ones that deliver you the lowest cost per sale. That's how you become third party free!

> To use our cost-per-sale calculator and to work out what you can actually afford to be spending to drive more direct custom, visit www.moredirectbookings.com/resources

GOOGLE REMARKETING / FACEBOOK RETARGETING

You might have heard of these terms; they've been around for 5-6 years or so (at the point of writing this book) and are used to expert effect by the OTAs to drive more business but are almost non-existent by individual hotel marketers. I can't tell you how many times I've sat across people who are responsible for the marketing of a hotel that haven't heard of Google Remarketing.

These traditionalists would sooner spend a four-figure sum to advertise online or offline, than allocate £25 per month on Google Remarketing – because they are ignorant of this new advertising technology that exists today.

Let me explain why this is wrong on every level.

Google Remarketing Explained

By its very nature, Google Remarketing allows you to re-market to people that have visited your website by advertising to these people across the Internet on a pay per click basis.

To put this another way, Google Remarketing will allow you to advertise, for free, on some of the world's biggest websites. Seriously. Go visit any major website and look for ads that have a little triangle in the top right hand corner – this is a Google ad. In these spaces, you will only see ads for websites that you have visited on the Internet browser you are using.

Test it yourself. Go to booking.com and search for your own hotel. Then open a new tab and visit a major news website or travel site like CNN.com or skyscanner.com. If not right away, you will start to see booking.com advertising in these spaces to you. They are targeting you – someone who has shown interested in staying in your hotel – and advertising your hotel to you for free, until of course you click on the ad, then they'll likely be paying a small fee (typically less than £1) to get you back to the booking.com site and secure your business.

Technically the above example is something known as Dynamic Remarketing – where you can target not just the business but specific products within the business to people who've visited specific web pages. So if you wanted to remarket to people who have visited yourhotel.com/weddings, you could do so with wedding-specific remarketing ads rather than generic ads about your hotel.

Facebook Retargeting Explained

Facebook Retargeting works in very much the same way, but on Facebook. So rather than those ads appearing across Google's display network on millions of different websites, those ads just appear on Facebook; both the news feed and on the right-hand side. (Key point, these elements are correct at the time of writing but Facebook has changed dozens of times over the course of its short lifespan and may be different at the time of your reading).

The big advantage that Facebook has over Google when it comes to remarketing your product is that Facebook will work over multiple devices. So if a prospective customer visits your website looking for their next short break at their work computer (and they logged into Facebook) your remarketing ads will appear on their phone and tablet. Whereas Google's Remarketing tends to work only on the computer you initially visited the website on.

Again, Facebook Retargeting is charged on a pay-per-click basis, so you won't be charged for impressions, only when people click on the ads that bring them back to your website.

Why Remarketing is so effective (and cost effective)?

There's no denying, or hiding from the fact that the booking decision process has changed drastically over the last 10 years. The hotel booker today has more choice than he/she has ever had in history. This dramatic increase in choice has led to two key factors affecting the eventual booking of a hotel:

- More deals, offers and discounts across the industry
- The decision making process has got longer

Simply put, it's got a lot more competitive out there and harder to command the rates you want for your rooms. In order to sell rooms at attractive rates, you need to instil a burning desire in your customer to choose you over a nearby competitor. What you really want is for every customer that is choosing between your hotel and 3 or 4 others for their next leisure break, is to book with you irrespective of the fact that you're 10% or 20% more expensive. Remarketing will work to help you stay front of mind in that process.

More importantly, it is the most cost effective advertising medium out there. Typically we'll allocate a maximum budget of £30 per month – and for that, we'll advertise our product somewhere between 20,000-30,000 times on some of the world's biggest websites, and get close to 100 extra clicks to our website from people who have been to us once before. In an average month, this will yield 3 new bookings, giving us a cost per sale of £10. Which, will typically be less than 3% of the booking's actual value. Cost-Per-Sale will be discussed in more detail later in the book, but as a percentage of the business we're paying to acquire the customer, 3% or even 10% is much, much better than any OTA will give you. And these ads are checked a couple of times per month, so the management is minimal.

How to set it up

Both Google Remarketing and Facebook Retargeting are relatively straight-forward to set up, but you may need some help adding the 'remarketing tag' to your website. This is a small amount of HTML code that can be easily pasted into the back-end of your website.

> For a step-by-step guide on how to get these two invaluable marketing tools up and running for your hotel, visit www.moredirectbookings.com/resources

LOCAL NON-RESIDENT DINING

Driving more non-resident diners into the hotel is something that most hotels' I've come into contact with find difficult. Typically, this is an area that has not made the leap into digital marketing and still largely depends on traditional formats – which is not necessarily a bad thing it must be said. I'm in no way against traditional forms of marketing, in fact I'm not wedded to any form – only those that I know I can measure and that have proven to work.

So, with this in mind, should you decide to use, or continue to use traditional, offline marketing channels to market your restaurant or bar, ensure that you use a tracking telephone number, and have a very clear call to action. If your marketing spend is turning into telephone rings, you'll know one way or the other whether it's not working, is not working enough to justify the cost, or is delivering in accordance with your expectations.

However, digital marketing has a role to play; in particular location targeted Facebook Ads. If you are the admin or editor of your hotel's Facebook page, login, and visit your page. If you are in a populated area, on the left hand side of the page, you will see a number in bold in the tens or even hundreds of thousands. Above will read something along the lines of 'Number of people you can reach within 5 miles of your business' and a big blue button that says 'Promote Local Business'.

If you don't see a number chances are your hotel is situated in a relatively rural location. It is still possible to do some effective location-based targeting but you might have go a little further than 5 miles to get a decent number of people to target.

The idea behind this is that by using some clever, location-based targeting you can create Facebook ads to get locals or locally-based tourists to come and dine in the restaurant or have a drink in the bar.

So let's imagine you have a 2 AA Rosette restaurant and typically cater for 45+ couples who enjoy well presented food in a relaxed setting. Then you might create a search criteria of the following:

Males & Females
45+
Speak English
Educated to Degree Level
Located within 5 miles of hotel

The ad might offer something along the lines of:

Plan to dine out in [location] tonight

[image of delicious looking dish, your logo, two rosettes and tracking telephone number]

X Hotel specialises in delicious food in a relaxed setting in [location]. Click image to view menu.

This ad will take them to a page showing your menu, with a telephone tracking number and call to action to 'check availability for tonight'.

Depending on your location, your cost per click for this ad will be pennies, not pounds, and by using the telephone tracking number, you'll soon be able to discern whether or not the ad is delivering a return. If it isn't you might need to tweak the image you use, the ad copy, or the search criteria.

This method will also work brilliantly well if your hotel is located in an area that is popular amongst international tourists.

Many of the hotels we work with in the likes of the Lake District, the Cotswolds or London have a large proportion of Japanese, French and German tourists. In these instances, we'll have the ad copy translated into the appropriate language and change the search criteria to target prospective customers in their own language on Facebook and drive them to a menu page, again translated in their own language. In a fiercely competitive market in the height of the summer season, just imagine the level of advantage this gives our hotels against their competitors who rely on footfall alone for the business!

Whilst the above points will help you to become proactive in driving more direct business with some clever targeting, be prepared to invest in working out what doesn't work before you start seeing genuine results; particularly when targeting international tourists. Here's a few pointers:

- The Chinese have their own social media networks, so Facebook will likely be less effective at targeting Chinese tourists
- Languages do not translate literally. Sticking the text into Google Translate will not do the job, you will need to find someone who can not only translate the copy for you, but someone who can suggest the best phrase that best matches what you are trying to say in English.
- Visit Fiverr.com and search for translators. Each 'gig' will only cost you $5 (USD) so it's worth paying someone to translate it, and paying someone else to check it.

For more information and step-by-step guides on how to set up Facebook Advertising to target locally based customers, visit www.moredirectbookings.com/resources

SEO CRITICAL IMPROVEMENTS

This book is not intended to give you advice on Search Engine Optimisation (SEO), mostly because by the time this book is published, the advice would likely be irrelevant or detrimental to your organic ranking on search engines due to the ever changing nature of the search engine algorithms.

However, in this short chapter, I will offer some basic advice to ensure that you're not losing traffic unnecessarily.

1. Mobile Friendly

On 21st April 2015, Google started penalising websites that are not mobile friendly. If your website is not mobile optimised, you're almost certainly losing out on business. To check this, type in "Google Mobile Friendly Tool" into Google and click on the first link. Paste your website address into the bar on the website and it will soon show you whether you have a mobile friendly website or not.

2. Understand where "critical improvements" are needed

Another handy tool we use for all of our hotel clients is to use a free website called www.lipperhey.com

This tool runs a free comprehensive analysis of your website and will give you a list of 'Critical Improvements' needed to maximise the amount of organic traffic to your website.

Typically most websites will have the odd critical improvement needed, and these are ordinarily easy to fix. We have an in-house coder within our agency, but you can find someone who will be able to fix the issues quickly and efficiently on fiverr.com

> For more advice on how to maximise your organic ranking, and how to find the right freelancers to fix any issues with your website, visit www.moredirectbookings.com/resources

CALL ANSWERING COMPANY

As you might have worked out by now, I'm a big fan of outsourcing jobs and tasks that would either be too expensive to have in-house or that can be achieved to a better or more skilled level outside of the business.

The same is true for answering the telephone. By the very nature of the reception, it is near impossible to answer every call. If you have one person on reception who is responsible for

a) Checking in guests
b) Checking out guests
c) Dealing with guest queries
d) Answering the telephone

... guess which one will be last on the priority list of the receptionist when 2 or more things happen at once? And yet, as previously referred to in the tracking telephone numbers chapter – there are only so many ways that you can drive direct bookings, and the phone is one of them. A big one at that.

One of the first things we do with every new client is ensure that they never, ever miss an opportunity to take a booking, so we have a call answering partner company who, 24 hours a day will answer the telephone in the name of the hotel if a phone call goes unanswered after 4 rings.

What's more; this company is briefed to answer the frequently asked questions as far as possible, and to take bookings by simply checking the availability online and taking payment over the phone and ordering online through the hotel's website.

In the instances where a query cannot be accommodated by the outsourced team, the customer is informed that they'll find the answer to the query and another member of the team will call them back shortly. In these cases, an email is sent to the appropriate member of the team instructing them to call the customer back with the answers to the specific query.

Typically, the call answering process will be answered by someone in the UK in the day, and re-routed to a New Zealand equivalent in the evenings. The system ensures that

  a) Every telephone call is answered by a real, native English-speaking person who is well informed to answer key questions about the hotel
  b) Bookings are never missed because the receptionist is busy

It is astounding how many hotels don't answer the phone when you call, and this simple call answering safety net is typically worth thousands to us in would-be-lost business every year.

In terms of cost, you'd be looking at somewhere between £0.80 - £1.20 per call answered which offers a nice opportunity to test the return on investment over a 2-3 month period. Chances are you'll find that it's a no-brainer marketing investment.

For a list of UK companies that offer this service and advice on how to effectively find and brief a call answering company, visit www.moredirectbookings.com/resources

CONTROLLING WHAT GOES ON YOUR TRIPADVISOR PAGE

Have you ever seen hotels on TripAdvisor who seem to have an incredible amount of top reviews and very few bad ones, and wonder how on earth they managed it?

Well, there's a combination of things that these hotels will be doing, but in these examples, you can guarantee that two things are happening:

1. The experience at that hotel is usually very good
2. They're proactively encouraging the good reviews and proactively discouraging the bad reviews.

At this point, I recommend taking a look at the TripAdvisor page of the Cranleigh Boutique, and you'll see what I mean.

Now, no matter what 'system' or 'process' you use to control your TripAdvisor page, two important points need to be made:

1. You cannot 100% control what goes on, and does not go on TripAdvisor
2. If your product is not consistently performing for your customers, then any time or money invested into improving your TripAdvisor page will likely be wasted.

On point number two, if you know that you're underwhelming a good percentage of your customers with poor service, tired rooms or anything else that your customers are regularly pointing out as a flaw in your business, implementing a review-influencing process will be like putting lipstick on a pig! And let's face it, if you're serious about driving more direct business, you should know by now that marketing the product is only half the battle; you have to deliver on your product too.

This aside, we use a cloud-based software called Review Filter with our hotels – and it's superb at filtering the good reviews from the bad. For a small monthly fee, it's an integral part of the businesses whom we market because like it or not TripAdvisor still continues to carry a great deal of influence on booking decisions.

Here's how it works:

1. On the day guests depart the hotel; they receive an email or a text from the General Manager or the owner of the hotel offering their thanks for staying, and a link to review the hotel.

2. That link takes recent customers to a blank page where the customer can leave a review, and rate the stay out of 5.

3. Here's where it gets clever: If the review is a 1, 2 or 3 star rating, the customer is redirected to a page that simply offers thanks for the review and apologies that expectations were not met. If however the review is 4 or 5 stars, they are taken to a separate page where they can easily copy the review they have just written and click on a link that takes them to hotel's TripAdvisor page.

4. If the customer gave a 4 or 5 star review but didn't make it as far as to click on the TripAdvisor link, they are automatically sent a reminder email 2 days later.

This system works because we know that typically customers will only review in one place. So if it's a scathing 1 star review, you're getting there first and having them vent their disapproval in a place where that won't damage the reputation of the property. If however it's a positive, glowing 5 star review, that's something you'd like to share online.

The key of course to all of this is, is consistency. With reservations systems where it's not currently possible for the departing guest data to pass seamlessly into the Review Filter account, we have a member of our team manually login, export the data each day and upload to Review Filter.

Over time, we typically see the TripAdvisor ranking improve as more positive reviews filter onto the page, and fewer negative reviews start to emerge. It's a slow burner this, and results should start to emerge after 3-6 months, but, as previously mentioned, TripAdvisor carries an inordinate amount of influence on your customer's booking decision, particularly when you are attracting international tourists so it's well worth the investment.

> For more information, and to claim a free trial, visit www.moredirectbookings.com/resources

VIDEO

At the time of writing this book, Facebook will give you 30% more views if you post a video, rather than just text or an image. You might have even noticed how much more video appears in your daily news feed on Facebook compared to a few years or even a few months ago.

Investing in video for your hotel is the way forward, and yet still very few hotels do it, let alone do it well. Which should scream OPPORTUNITY to you as a hotelier who is prepared to do what it takes to reduce your dependency on the OTAs. At the time of writing this, The Cranleigh Boutique has well over 100,000 Facebook Likes, and much of that is using video to bring our product to life.

Now, when it comes to video, most hotels will have a 4 or 5 minute video completed, stick it on YouTube, embed it on the website and forget about it. This is no longer good enough.

You would be far better making ten 30-second videos than one 5 minute one. However I would strongly advice 25 videos minimum. This will involve having a videographer into the hotel for 1 or 2 days, and creating a video for all of the selling points you have at the hotel, all of the different room-types and several staff interviews and customer interviews. Here's an overview on what you should have to effectively make use of video to market your hotel:

General Video
Including shots of exterior, communal areas, a couple of bedrooms and dining area.

Room Type Videos
Each room type should have it's own video
Staff video
Ask the staff why they love working for your hotel
Customer video
Ask the customers what they enjoyed about your hotel
Restaurant video
Interview with the head chef and panning shots of the restaurant
Key Selling Point Videos
Things like being pet friendly, having AA rosettes, being just 2 minutes from the town centre etc.
Occasion videos
Weddings / Anniversaries / Birthdays – these videos are designed to convey clearly why your hotel would make the perfect choice for the customer's special occasion.

The thing to remember is that prospective customers will typically not watch a video more than 60 or 90 seconds, so by focusing on some of the key selling points, you can really hammer home why choosing your hotel is the best one for their needs. Plus, if you stop and give real thought to the way in which couples choose a hotel, unless it's a surprise for a partner, your hotel will be found by one half of the partnership and that person then needs to be sold on why this hotel is the best choice. Then once this has happened, the customer will have to sell the idea of this hotel to their partner and explain why they think your hotel is the best choice. A video will do this better than anything else, and can be easily shared on Facebook. Every time a video is posted on the Facebook wall of a hotel we manage, our objective is always to maximise the amount of shares we get from this video.

Now when it comes to cost, it doesn't have to be outrageously expensive but it also shouldn't be cheap. Having a videographer into the hotel for the day will likely set you back about £750 and perhaps the same again to have them edited professionally.

For advice on find and hiring a professional videographer and video editor, as well as a detailed strategy for creating and promoting your videos, go to
www.moredirectbookings.com/resources

AUTOMATED BIRTHDAY EMAILS

As will be discussed in PART TWO of this book, email marketing is all about relevance. The more information you have about your previous and prospective customers, allows to you send more relevant communications via email and other channels.

This statement is at it's most pertinent for Birthdays and Anniversaries. This is the time when the people who subscribe to your emails, like you on Facebook, or have shown engagement in your product in some other fashion are likely to be most receptive to a carefully crafted sales message from you.

Importantly, most CRM (customer relationship management) systems, will allow you to automate emails on specific dates, so that once you have acquired this all important data, you can automatically trigger a set of emails that encourages your prospective or previous customers to once again engage with your product and, have their desire to visit reignited by the fact that they have a special occasion on the horizon.

Creating a Facebook Competition

This is where; again, Facebook is the perfect medium for this. Much of the success of the 100,000+ Facebook likes we achieved at the Cranleigh Boutique is down to creating super attractive competition prizes and targeting entry of those competitions at people who we think would be most likely to visit us. Now Facebook's rules and regulations around competitions changes regularly.

> For the most up to date Facebook Competition rules, visit www.moredirectbookings.com/resources

So as a starting point, we tend to use a helpful tool called TabFoundry.com. It's a paid for tool that allows you to create competitions adhering to Facebook's most up to date rules and regulations using the provided templates. For one Facebook page, you'll be looking at a cost of about $9 (USD) per month for access to it. Within this easy to navigate system, you'll be able to create a custom-looking competition tab that requires the following information from the entrant to enter the competition:

First Name
Last Name
Email
Date of Birth (no year required)
Anniversary (no year required)

A few pointers on these data capture fields:

- Always ask for first name and last name in separate fields. This is because you'll want to personalise the email to the competition entrant, and it tends to be a lot easier if these two names are in separate fields.
- Make sure you list the date of birth field as listed above. By specifying that no year is required will increase your sign-ups as some people may feel sensitive of the fact they are giving you their full date of birth.
- Ensure that all fields apart from Anniversary are marked as 'required' fields – you don't want to find that you have 1,000 entrants and only 50 date of births! Similarly, not everyone has an anniversary, so this should not be a required field.

Maximising Entries

Once you have created your competition, make sure you have at least a month or so for which to promote it. To maximise the amount of entries you'll want to use every medium available to you. This will include

Facebook posts
Facebook boosted posts
Email
At Reception

You want as many entries as humanly possible. There's a few reason for this:

1. If you, for example achieve 1,000 entries, you will broadly have 3 automated emails being sent every day – that's 21 per week and over 80 a month. That's a fair number of engaged prospective customers who will be receiving a timely, relevant offer to come and stay in your hotel.
2. However, it's not all rosy. Approx. only 20-30% of those emails will get opened. And of those that open the emails, over 99% won't book.

In short, this is a numbers game. You need to do everything you can do maximise the amount of entrants you receive to ensure you can get a handful of bookings from this marketing activity.

Completing & Automating

Once the competition has come to an end, you'll want to inform the lucky winner, and get that data plugged into your CRM as soon as you can. Typically we will automate four emails at the following times:

Email 1 – Three weeks before key date – present offer
Email 2 – 3 days later – reminder
Email 3 – 10 days before key date – 2nd reminder
Email 4 – on day of key date – happy birthday/anniversary

> For template emails of what we send to customers, visit www.moredirectbookings.com/resources

If your CRM does not speak directly with your reservations system, it will be worth checking in once a week to see who has booked under this offer so that they can be removed from the remainder of the campaign.

Is it worth it?

You might be thinking that it might sound like an awful lot of work if the outcome is a handful of bookings… Well, this marketing activity will not make you rich. But I've included it in the book because these small marginal gains marketing campaigns will help you to reduce your dependency on the OTAs.

Sadly, if there is a silver bullet to driving more direct bookings, I've not found it. Rather, this is a simple example of a low (or no) cost marketing campaign to capture data, nurture the prospective customers and push a relevant sales message when they are likely to be receptive to one. If done well, it will drive a few more bookings each month, commission free.

FACEBOOK DATA UPLOAD & LOOKALIKE AUDIENCES

Again, this is one of the least known marketing tools available to hotels, but it can be so effective at maximising the takings from an email campaign.

On Facebook, you have the ability to perform two key tasks:

1. Upload your database to Facebook
2. Find a lookalike audience to your current list of customers

Let's start with the first – uploading your database to Facebook. You might be wondering what tangible benefit this would offer you. Well to really understand the benefit of this tool, we have to go back to understanding the decision making process. You see, if you are attempting to encourage your prospective or previous customers to visit you and spend several hundred pounds, you need to give them a very good reason to do that (which does not necessarily need to be price related) and essentially you need to interrupt them from daily life, take them off auto-pilot and have them think actively about your hotel.

One of the most effective ways of doing this is to take a given message and push it across multiple media. So let's imagine that you run a 3-day flash sale to the whole email database and over 3 days, you send 3 or 4 emails to encourage sales of that flash sale.

(As a side point, you might think this sounds like an excessive amount of emails to send in 3 days – the issue of 'customer bombardment' will be covered in PART TWO but for now, all I'll

mention is that these types of campaigns continue to be the best performing email campaigns we run for any hotel, and the cumulative amount of business yielded from emails 2, 3 and 4 almost always is more than the total created from email 1)

Now, imagine for a moment that instead of communicating this message just through the medium of email, you doubled up the message on Facebook and via text message, for example. Well, if you're that prospective customer you'd do well not notice this 3-day sale! And let's face it; if the offer goes unnoticed, you don't get the business.

So how do you target people on Facebook? You can upload your database to Facebook. Essentially what you'll be doing here is identifying which of the emails on your database are associated with a Facebook account – meaning that you push Facebook ads at them, irrespective of whether they like your hotel's Facebook page or not. This is effective because it will allow you amplify the sales message across multiple media, increasing your chances of converting the browsers into buyers.

But you also have something known as lookalike audiences on Facebook. Let's say for example you have 5,000 Facebook Likes – these might be a mixture of previous customers and people who just like the look of your product. Any sales message or data capture campaign you might want to push can be targeted at a lookalike audience. That is to suggest people of a similar age, location and educational background as those people who currently like your page.

This is a very useful tool for growing your online following of people most likely to be interested in your product.

> Because the location of these tools tend to change on Facebook regularly, rather than explain in words how to do this in this book, you'll find an up-to-date step-by-step guide at www.moredirectbookings.com/resources

PART TWO:
18 THINGS YOU NEED TO KNOW ABOUT EMAIL MARKETING

INTRODUCTION

Firstly, no you've not misread this—yes, there really are 18 things I have to say about email marketing. The reason there are so many is that without question, email marketing is the most important, most immediate source of direct bookings available to the independent hotelier. Now, you might disagree. You might have tried it, dabbled with email marketing and have come to the conclusion that it doesn't work for your hotel. Well if that's you, great news! Because I can say with absolute certainty that email marketing WILL work for your hotel, provided you use the 18 approaches listed in this section of the book. Or to put it another way, unless you use these 18 things, you'll continue to receive mediocre results. On the other hand, you may have been doing ok with email marketing—it works, somewhat inconsistently, but it does ok. Well great, these 18 things will help you improve those numbers. I'm conscious that before discussing the 18 points, as with any good marketing campaign, we need to clearly define what we are trying to achieve—the marketing objectives, if you will.

So when you send out an email, you should be trying to achieve these three things, in this order:
1. Get the email opened.
2. Get the email read.
3. Get the recipient to take some form of action as a direct result of reading your email.

In 99% of the cases with email marketing, these are your objectives. Remember them whenever you set yourself down to craft a new email. A good point to note too is that objective 3--encouraging action--should be clearly defined. Now it might be as simple as 'make a reservation'. Call to check availability. It might be 'click on a link'. Whatever it is, be clear in your mind as to what you want the recipient to do.

1. SUBJECT LINE

I shudder when I see the word "newsletter" in a subject line. The subject of an email is one of the most, if not *the most* important element of an email. Take yourself back to the three objectives. Objectives 2 and 3 (reading the email and taking action) don't happen unless objective 1 (opening the email) happens. The subject line should do two things to achieve objective 1:

a) Create intrigue and curiosity.
b) Be related, someway, to the content of the email.

We human beings are fickle creatures; we like things that intrigue and entertain us. Like a moth drawn to a flame, your recipients will be drawn to something that sparks interest and curiosity within them. The subject line "April Newsletter" screams "Unimportant" and "Don't read me"—well if the email isn't being read, what's the point of sending it!?

However, a weird and wonderful subject line that fails to correlate with the body of the email can do harm. A wonderfully intriguing subject line followed by dry, dreary and unrelated content will frustrate the recipient and make them think twice before opening another of your emails. They'll think they've been lured under false pretences and in some small way, conned into reading your email.

Another important point here is that subject lines should not summarise the content of the email. Too often I see things like this drop into my inbox:

20% off Spring Breaks, New Restaurant Menu & Our Recent Breakfast Award!

This is a typical mistake made in hotel email marketing—summarising the entire concept of the email. In a business 1:1 context, that's the expected norm—using a subject line that directly relates to the body. "Mr. Smith's Invoice" sent to Julie in accounts. "Faulty TV in room 108" sent to Andrew in maintenance, "Your Vegan Dietary Requirements" sent to Mr. and Mrs. Jones coming to stay later that week. It all makes sense and it's been hard-wired into us. BUT THIS IS NOT MARKETING. These are examples of functional day-to-day correspondence with staff, suppliers and customers.

The difference is simply that your marketing messages are not there to inform; they are there to interrupt the recipients' day with something of interest, to build and nurture the relationship with that recipient so they feel positive feelings toward your hotel and take some (albeit small at first) action that demonstrates a level of engagement. BUT—none of that stuff happens unless you first build intrigue. So a summarising subject line like the example offered previously is effectively saying to the recipient—"I know you're busy, but would you like to know about our offer we're running? Can I interrupt you for a few moments to tell you about our new menu? Is what you're doing right this second more important than our new breakfast award?"

Sure a few people will take a look, but chances are people really don't care enough about your hotel to stop what they're doing and find out about things you deem important . . . unless you build intrigue in that subject line.

It's been mentioned previously but it's worth reiterating: everything covered in this book I've already used to great success in my own hotel and other businesses —visit wowhotelmarketing.com and subscribe to my emails and you'll receive weekly examples using clever subject lines that get your emails opened and read.

Additionally, download my list of "Tried and Tested Subject Lines" by visiting www.moredirectbookings.com/resources

2. DUAL READERSHIP PATH

So you've crafted an intriguing but relevant subject line and managed to get the email opened. Great, let's move to objective number 2—getting the thing read. Because all that's happened so far is the recipient has allowed himself or herself to be seduced for a microsecond by intrigue and curiosity. If that curiosity is met with continuous prose, the recipient is likely to disengage because big chunks of text is not easy on the eye and requires concentrated effort. This is where a dual readership path comes in. Simply put, a dual readership path allows the reader to skim and quickly get the gist of the email's content. Think of it like this: every person whom you send a marketing email to probably doesn't want it in their inbox. So when you've somehow--through sheer dumbfounded curiosity—encouraged them to open that email you sent, they are asking themselves subconsciously, "Why should I read this?" and if they can't find a very good answer, normally within the first seven seconds, sometimes less, they will disengage and you've lost them.

So the trick is to use a side column and highlight the key aspects of the content in bold text that's significantly bigger than the main copy. Let them cast their eyes over your email and within a few seconds their question of, "Why should I read this email?" should be answered well enough to continue reading.

> Great examples of dual readership paths from emails that have delivered over £50,000 in sales in a matter of days are provided at www.moredirectbookings.com/resources

3. DATABASE SEGMENTATION

Segmentation of your database is essential. Email marketing at its most basic level is about relevance. A message that's relevant will get read 100 times more often than an irrelevant message—that might sound a bit obvious but it's an important point to make when you consider the process of what's going through the recipient's mind—"What's in it for me?" "Why should I bother reading this?" and "Is this worth my valuable time?"

An irrelevant message will cause the recipient to conclude that it's not worth reading, or even opening. So, with that stated, segmentation is crucial, and it works in many ways.

A) [Firstname] or [Title] [Last Name]

This is the most important segmentation point. How you address the recipient is vital and chances are your database will be split between those data records that have just the 'first name', 'initial' and 'last name', and 'no name'. In almost all cases of working with hotels, this tends to be the case. So, in the process of sending out email correspondence, you'll normally want to send two batches. The first addressing the firstnamers e.g., "Dear John" and the second addressed to the secondnamers e.g., "Dear Mr. Smith."

Remember that the purpose of this piece of communication is to engage and build a relationship with the recipient to the point where they take some action e.g. make a booking, etc. You don't get much more personal than the customer's name, so it is perilous to use the wrong name and/or wrong address.

B) The Customer Lifecycle

Not all customers are in the same place when it comes to their involvement with your business. Consider, and give careful thought to the fact that there are customers in your existing database who:

1. Stayed over 2 years ago and might be considering their next break
2. Stayed less than a month ago
3. Have already made a booking for a future date
4. Have had a bad experience in your hotel
5. Have stayed over 10 times in the last 5 years

These 5 customer types have very different relationships and perceptions of your hotel and they are in different stages in the buying cycle. In marketing terms you might say that each of these customers is at different stages in the sales funnel—the key point being that if you send out a generic, "Buy now" message to everyone, the relevance suffers. The initial perception might be something like this:

1. That's interesting.
2. Why are they sending me another offer, I only just left!
3. I wonder if this offer is better than what I just paid.
4. Stop spamming me.
5. Despite being a loyal customer, I don't feel I'm being given preferential treatment.

To combat this irrelevance and annoyance and the threat of spam complaints, we adopt a basic level of segmentation to ensure that messages are as relevant as possible. It's adopted by the Seth Godin approach as outlined in his book *Purple Cow*, and it works like this:

1. Prospects—subscribed but never stayed.
2. Recent Customers—stayed within the last 3 months.

3. Non-Recent Customers—stayed between 3 and 18 months ago.
4. Loyal Customers—stayed twice or more in the last 18 months.
5. Former Customers—stayed but not in the last 18 months.

Now that we have a basic level of segmentation, we can start thinking about what the core message and objective should be for each segment:

Type of Customer	Message	Objective
1. Prospects	Look how great a short break at our hotel could be for you	Get them to book
2. Recent Customers	Thank you for your business	Have the customer feel that their hard-earned cash was well invested in a hotel that truly valued its custom
3. Non-Recent Customers	Here are all the reasons why you should come again	Repeat Booking
4. Loyal Customers	Thank You	Repeat purchase and acknowledgment of being a priority customer
5. Former Customer	We Miss You	Get them to return

C) Food/accommodation

You may also have a strong non-resident F&B (Food & Beverage) arm to your business. You may then, for example, have a completely different segment of your database that resides within a 25-mile radius of the hotel, and you'll only want to send them news and offers about the restaurant. Start sending these recipients' messages about booking a short break and you'll soon start to see these people disengage from these irrelevant messages.

Having said that, the referral business is an often-overlooked opportunity. These regular dining customers might occasionally require accommodation for visiting friends and family, so the occasional reference to this could help keep your hotel front of mind when they're looking.

D) Future Bookings

Lastly, and arguably the segment most influential on sales revenue is the list of customers who have a booking for a date in the future. If you send these customers an offer that is a better rate than they originally booked for, you'll find yourself quickly losing money as well as the customers' trust in your ability to provide a great service. Omitting these people from any sales messages makes good financial and relationship-building sense because whilst you don't want to have to refund the difference in rates paid and offered, you'll also want to be careful not to ask someone who has just bought to buy again and buy again—not good for the relationship.

My final point on segmentation is to dispel the perception that rather than broadcasting one email, you now need to send about 25 to each segment—this simply isn't the case. Typically, with this sophisticated level of segmentation, all that's required is to create one email and tweak the copy to ensure relevance. Bear in mind also that you're doing very well if 3 in 10 people read your email, so making that first sentence relevant to the individual should normally do the trick. For example, your email to a loyal customer might start:

Dear [first name]
As a loyal customer of XXX hotel . . .

Similarly a former customer might receive the message below:

Dear [firstname]
It's been awhile since you visited us at XXX hotel.

And a Recent Customer might receive something like:

Dear [firstname]
Thank you for your recent booking at XXX hotel.

These subtle changes will make all the difference in achieving the three core objectives of getting it opened, getting it read and getting the customer to take the desired action.

For more detailed information on how to effectively segment your database to improve your direct business created from email marketing, visit www.moredirectbookings.com/resources

4. WHOM THE EMAIL IS SENT 'FROM'

Let's venture back to our first objective: get the email opened. In equal measure to the subject line, the person who is perceived to have sent the email influences this objective. Remember also that this medium is first and foremost designed to strengthen your relationship with your customers and prospective customers. And the easiest way of strengthening, or indeed building a relationship is to be personal, engaging and, fundamentally, real!

This is why it is so important to personify your sender as much as possible to ensure they are not just another name in a steadily-filling inbox. You'll not only want to use the individual's name, you'll want to bring them to life through the screen. You'll want their personality to leap out at the customer. In the way that charisma draws people to engage and listen when someone is speaking, email personality and charisma works the same way.

This idea is akin to the notion of stories—people like stories. They love the drama, the beginning, middle and end. They enjoy depicting the story in their own mind, and bringing it to life. And if you start to build and paint this story in your recipient's mind, having the email come from "Hotel Name" or even worse "Reservations" or "Marketing"(!) completely and utterly limits the engagement level. Any story you share, any image you paint in the recipient's mind and any feelings you evoke will take the recipient one step further to opening their wallets or purses and booking a short break at your hotel—this is infinitely harder to do without some level of personal interaction.

When a real person sends an email, they have sat at a computer, thought, written, rewritten, punched away at a keyboard until they were happy to broadcast their message. When the email comes from a generic entity like, "Hotel Name" or a certain department of the hotel like, "Reservations" it is devoid of any personal element.

Let's look at this another way: when your customer calls the hotel, he or she is greeted by a friendly voice ready to help (or at least they should be). When they arrive at the hotel, a warm smile and personable member of staff should greet and welcome them. The very basics of the essence of hospitality are: be friendly and welcoming. And yet in my experience, most hotels adopt the most corporate and impersonal approach when they approach customers via email—it's bonkers!

My last point—if you remain unconvinced about this: it is important to split-test. Split your database into a random 50:50. Send one email from [Hotel Name]. Send one email from a specific person. Keep the subject line, the message and the time of delivery exactly the same. Do this 2 or 3 times and I'm certain you'll see that personal emails are more likely to be opened than impersonal ones.

> To access my "Quick Start To Successful Email Check List" visit www.moredirectbookings.com/resources

5. WHOM THE EMAIL IS SENT 'TO'

Whom the email is addressed to is important because it's the first thing the reader is likely to see, and because it's so personal to the recipient. Wherever possible address the email to [first name] or [title] [surname]. I've not come across a database yet where the data was so organised that all three columns (first, last and title) were all intact. Almost every email we send for every client is sent twice—once to 'first-namers' and once to 'title-lastnamers'. Which means it is vitally important to segment your database into groups or tags as to which email they should receive.

Again thinking about our goal of building a relationship with these customers, if you arrived for a meeting or an interview and used the wrong name for the person you were meeting, it wouldn't get things off to a great start.

I won't labour this point; I'll only say that failing to merge an accurate name into the email will significantly hinder your chances of building a strong relationship with your recipient, which in turn minimises your chance of selling to them.

> To access my "Quick Start To Successful Email Check List" visit www.moredirectbookings.com/resources

6. EMAIL ENGAGEMENT STRATEGY

An email engagement strategy is simply the tone of the email; the voice you use to communicate with your audience. This is an area of email marketing often overlooked. Often the design and the aesthetic are given more weight in the sender's mind than the copy. This is a fundamental mistake. The tone of voice you use is more influential than the way the email looks when it comes to getting the email read.

So when I see no greeting and an email is image-led with a short sentence under each image relating to whatever is being promoted and sold—the email might look slick and clean but it's far from being engaging. Worse still is when those words read like marketing speak! Completely bonkers. Chances are your customer doesn't want to be sold to, doesn't want to be marketed to, and therefore gains no enjoyment from reading sentences like:

Why not join us for a relaxing break this weekend at our sensual spa?

This sentence screams sales, and really bad salesmanship at that. Remember that the fundamental point of email marketing is to engage, build a relationship and encourage the sale. Well, this sentence does none of these, if anything it discourages the sale through lack of creativity and non-reader centric words like *us* and *our*. A much better approach would be:

If you're finding yourself a little stressed, and maybe thinking that you could really do with some time off, then the sensual spa at x hotel will give you the relaxing break you need this weekend.

Notice how much more reader focused this is as opposed to being sender-focused. The word *you* features five times. The spa at the hotel is referenced in the third person changing the dynamic of the conversation from, "Buy from me" to "Spend your money here" which, although subtle, is a much more powerful sales tool. Most importantly perhaps, this approach is seemingly coming from *a real person*. That's the entire point of email marketing—build a relationship so that the sender is more likely to buy when they're ready.

One of my favourite examples is one of our clients at Wow Guest Hotel Marketing – a country house hotel in Scotland. We have created a carefully thought-out email engagement strategy that has delivered literally tens of thousands of revenue from a small database. This hotel is in the South West Scotland and is one of the most beautiful country house hotels you will ever visit; it's family run, in the heart of the countryside and the old building is set in acres of beautifully landscaped gardens. Now, being pet-friendly is a big selling point for this hotel, and they have their own Golden Retriever called Roxy.

> To see an example of a 'Roxy' email that has successfully delivered sales, visit www.moredirectbookings.com/resources

We send at least one email per month, and it delivers sales every month. I must give credit to the owner of the hotel who thought I was mad at this suggestion but decided to go with it anyway. For this small independent hotel in Scotland, email marketing has delivered well over £20,000 in a few short months from a database of little more than 400 previous customers.

Now in terms of engagement, it couldn't be higher. Regularly responding emails come through from guests sharing their affection and enjoyment for these emails and it's also not uncommon for a guest to respond as their dog! I'm told that almost every guest that visits is desperate to meet Roxy! This light-hearted approach has evoked feelings of humour and enjoyment with readers and combined with a superb product, they've encouraged a great deal of repeat custom.

Just to be clear, I'm not endorsing a light-hearted, tongue-in-cheek approach to your email marketing, or that you should find your nearest pet and start punching away at the keyboard writing as if you were them. No, this approach works for this particular hotel because it's relevant and appropriate. The point I am highlighting here is that finding a tone of voice that's engaging, that's suitable and consistent for your hotel will serve you better than dry, dull, salesy text that leaves the reader feeling nothing.

7. TRACKING TELEPHONE NUMBERS

Tracking telephone numbers seem to be the most underused (but absolutely essential) marketing tool in the hotel industry. Giving customers multiple ways to engage with you is sensible. What you're effectively doing is making it easier for the customer to interact with the hotel by allowing them to choose the medium of their preference. So whilst you should encourage customers to "Book online" you should also encourage customers to "Email us for more details" and "Call to check availability"—the more ways to interact and get in touch the better.

With this in mind, when your third objective of your email is to get the recipient to take some action, ensure that a tracking telephone number is used. I covered this earlier in the book, but to clarify, a tracking telephone number is simply a local number that redirects to your desired telephone number (e.g. the front desk) allowing you to track how many calls are being received and how many calls are being left unanswered.

Importantly then, within the context of email marketing, different messages or different segments should be assigned different numbers ... which leads me nicely onto split-testing…

> To access my "Quick Start To Successful Email Check List" visit www.moredirectbookings.com/resources

8. SPLIT TESTING

Split-testing is the means to improve your marketing by testing segments of your market or database with multiple variants of the same or similar messages. So let's say then, for example, that you're thinking about promoting a "3 nights for the price of 2" offer or a "33% off"—and you're not sure which one to go with, and ultimately are unsure as to which offer will resonate and perform better with the database. So you send both. Two different randomly selected segments of the database get an email—both identical with the only differences being that one's pushing 3 for 2 and another's pushing 33% off, and importantly, a separate tracking number has been set up for each, allowing you to assess which offer made the phone ring more! And just to be clear, these two tracking telephone numbers would ordinarily divert to the same phone line.

Split-testing separates the well-intentioned 'good marketing' from the successful 'great marketing'. There's often this common misconception that marketing is simply about finding the right ways to promote your business and avoiding the wrong ways. There are undoubtedly wrong ways to send emails if your objective is engagement and sales. But when it comes to the much-sought-after correct way of achieving these objectives, it's much more complicated; suffice to say there's a long list of things to do and not to do, but finding "the best" way of doing things to achieve your objectives takes time and patience and most notably a great deal of split-testing.

Within the realms of email marketing, the things to split test to achieve the best possible result are as follows:

- subject line

- time and day of delivery
- offer type
- style

The things to measure then may well be things like open rates, click-through rates, number of phone calls received, number of bookings taken. Before any split-test, you should ascertain what you are testing and the method you will use to measure. For example, sending one batch at 8 am and another at 8 pm to ascertain the receptiveness of the message at these times of day would typically be measured by both open and click-through rates. The context behind this might be that whilst recipients were more likely to open the email when it dropped in their inbox first thing, they might be less likely to engage further (i.e. click-through to the website) at the start of the day, than at the end of the day. That's why you would split-test to maximise engagement.

One big warning comes with split-testing, and it's a bit obvious, but I see it happening far too frequently—only change one thing at a time! I've seen countless marketers and hoteliers split test emails with a different subject line, a different time of delivery and a different message to see which one performs better. Well this practise is just about as pointless as it gets because whilst you achieved a better performing email, how on earth do you know which element of variation helped you achieve that better performance? So test one thing at a time.

Most CRM (Customer Relationship Management) systems will have a split-test which is sometimes referred as, an "A/B testing" feature. It is important to note that this test should be a random segment. There's really very little point testing a special offer against customers versus prospects in your database because the relationship these two have with your hotel is completely different.

My penultimate point on this topic is that perhaps the most

critical reader of this book may think... why? What's the point? Is it not just creating extra work for me? And to this point my answer is simply—don't split-test for the sake of it, but if you can find an insight into your database that will allow you to engage with them better in the future, then you should absolutely do it. For example, split-testing these two subject lines probably won't deliver much insight to steer you in the future:

Split-test A
"Lots to do this summer at [hotel name]"

Split-test B
"So much to do this summer at [hotel name]"

All you're changing in the instance above is a variation of the same meaning which I dare say won't help you achieve better engagement and sales next time you come to send an email. However the following example might...

Split-test A
"Lots to do this summer at [hotel name]."

Split-test B
"[first name], there's lots to do this summer at [hotel name]."

Effectively what you're trying to ascertain is whether merging the recipient's first name into the subject of the email will encourage a higher open and click-through rate. This would be something worth knowing for future broadcasts.

Lastly, if you have a database of a significant size, and I would say if you have at least 10,000 emails, you can sample test. Take a random selection of 1,000 email addresses and send split-test A. Then take another random selection of 1,000 emails and send split-test B. After a couple of days, analyse the results based on the core objective of what you were trying to achieve, and send the winner out to the further 8,000. This is a more immediate form of split-testing and is one of the easiest things to do to maximise the level of engagement and sales achieved.

To access my "Quick Start To Successful Email Check List" visit www.moredirectbookings.com/resources

9. UNOPENED RE-SEND

If you do nothing with these proven techniques, do this. It's quite possibly the easiest thing you can do with email marketing and will guarantee more people engaging with your email, and very often (if you've done much of the other stuff well) more sales.

Here's what you do:
1. Send an email out.
2. Twenty-four hours later resend the same email to everyone that didn't open it with a different subject line.

It doesn't get much simpler than that!

This works because people are busy and inboxes are crowded places. If the recipient only gets to their inbox 4 or 5 hours after you sent the email, chances a great bulk of emails would have amassed on top of your all important message, and probably from senders they deem far more important and significant like family members, friends and colleagues. So if you're fighting for attention with emails containing new pictures of siblings' nieces and nephews, important instructions from the boss, weekend plans from the best friend—in those cases, the chances of your recipient getting around to seeing, opening, reading and engaging with your email are dramatically reduced.

This is no exaggeration by the way. These very important people and messages are your competition. You're all fighting for the attention of your recipient, and even the best-written, most beautifully designed, most relevant message from a hotel doesn't stand a chance against emails from the family, the boss or from close friends. So with this in mind, if it doesn't get read within 24 hours, for whatever reason, send it again, but this time with a different subject line. Typically this simple practice will add another 5-10% more recipients opening your email and occasionally results in a few more sales too. And with a decent CRM system, it's a 3-minute job.

To access my "Quick Start To Successful Email Check List" visit www.moredirectbookings.com/resources

10. TIME OF DELIVERY

This topic was touch on in the split-testing section, but it greatly influences your ability to achieve our three main objectives which are the following:

1. Get the email opened.
2. Get the email read.
3. Get the recipient to take some form of action as a direct result of reading your email.

In most instances, the people who receive your email will have a personal and a work email address. If it's a work email address that you captured in your database, a common trend is that sending at lunch time or after 4 pm will yield better results in terms of open rates as this is ordinarily the time when office workers tend to be less productive and less focused on their work. (Just to be clear, you might find something completely different—this generic example is merely a trend I've seen with broadcasts sent to work email addresses.) Now, if most of the email addresses in your database are the customers' work email addresses, you might find that sending broadcasts out at either 12:30 pm or 4 pm Monday to Friday are the best performing times.

Similarly, a common trend tends to be that personal emails get read in the evening and on weekends. So if your emails are mostly being sent to customers' personal email addresses, then you might find that these times perform best for you.

As someone who subscribes to an inordinate amount of hotel emails, I can unequivocally say that Friday afternoons are the busiest time for hotel email broadcasts, most commonly by big groups and chains of hotels. Now this will be (one would hope) because their marketing team has identified that this time and day of broadcasting their message yields the best results through various levels of split-testing.

What this might indeed mean for you is that you really don't want to be fishing in the part of the river where the much bigger rods are taking all the fish. Stand out. Don't place yourself in the Friday afternoon race for attention; turn up unannounced where there's not another hotel in sight and tell them how great you are.

To access my "Quick Start To Successful Email Check List" visit www.moredirectbookings.com/resources

11. MULTIPLE FOLLOW-UP

Perhaps the single biggest thing impacting your sales is lack of follow-up. Most hoteliers I speak with have had mediocre results from email marketing, typically because they send out one email with a sales message and wait for the phone to ring. Well there's a common saying amongst marketers: "The worst number in marketing is one." The reality is that people are busy and you and your message are unimportant. That's why you have to follow up. Now I'm not talking about scattergun bombardment here, far from it. But if you've got a sales message you think your customers should know about, make sure you let them know! Shout it from the high heavens and shout it multiple times.

Without question, the most successful email campaigns we have designed and broadcast were for hotels that delivered fewer sales on email 1 than the cumulative effect of emails 2, 3 and 4.

> To access my "Quick Start To Successful Email Check List" visit www.moredirectbookings.com/resources

12. MULTIPLE CALLS TO ACTIONS

When you give real, careful thought to what specifically it is you want to achieve (the specific objective or outcome), it provides you with the means to construct an email that's far more likely to generate the desired response. So, for example, if the desired response is to click through to the website, then hiding the hyperlink at the bottom of the email is unlikely to yield great results. However, if within the copy you encourage and direct the reader to CLICK HERE multiple times, then your chances of achieving strong results for your desired response go up dramatically.

Similarly, if you want to encourage phone calls, make it super clear what the telephone number is and that you want the recipient of your email to call. Spell it out; leaving them with no shadow of doubt what it is you want them to do. Here's a simple rule you should adopt when planning the email:

Work out what you want them to do. Tell them. Tell them again. Remind them what you told them.

It might sound simple and repetitive but it works.

> To access my "Quick Start To Successful Email Check List" visit www.moredirectbookings.com/resources

13. ENCOURAGE UNSUBSCRIBES

This might seem counter-productive. Why would you ever want to encourage unsubscribes? There seems to be a tendency I've noticed within hoteliers to try to please everyone. I suppose it's human nature but by the nature of what you do, you're there to please, impress and be hospitable. Well, leave the hotelier hat at the door, and put your marketing hat on, because you're now marketing a business and it's your job to ascertain who of the people receiving your emails will almost certainly never return to your hotel; those for whom with even the best will in the world, will never buy from you again, will never recommend a friend or family member to visit no matter how hard you try and incentivise. Acknowledgment that these types of people exist in your database is the first step—because they do, without question.

Now the second step is to acknowledge exactly what your job is with these emails. The sad truth is that however big your open rates, however much people say they love reading your emails, if they ain't selling, they ain't working! (And yes I'm aware that throughout this book I've talked about how important engagement is--without question this is true--but the most important end goal is selling more rooms.)

So with this in mind, the question that every hotel marketer has to ask themselves is what's more important: selling rooms, or not annoying a few people that would never buy?

To put it another way, if you want to ensure that the unsubscribe rate is as low as it can be, your sales will suffer. Do not brush over this point; this statement is incontrovertible.

Now, back to this point about encouraging unsubscribes—why would you ever do this? Well, it comes down to that annoying little thing called Spam. You see, if you no longer wish to be a recipient of a certain email sender, then you have two options – "unsubscribe" or "report as spam." If a recipient unsubscribes, your email account remains untarnished, but with one fewer recipient for future broadcasts. If a recipient reports your email as spam, your "online reputation" takes a bit of a dent. Too many spam complaints and your emails will start to become blacklisted and become more susceptible to end up in the spam or junk folder. This is a problem because if you remember our three objectives for any email, (get it opened, get it read, get the desired action) if you take objective number one: "get it opened", your chances of achieving this objective decrease significantly if the recipient doesn't even see the email!

So with all this in mind, in preparation for a sales offer that you're keen to push, offering a fantastic deal that you're certain your customers should know about, it makes sound marketing sense to encourage unsubscribes, to reduce the spam complaints with that first email.

> To access my "Quick Start To Successful Email Check List" visit www.moredirectbookings.com/resources

14. PRE-HEADER

A pre-header is worth adding in above a leading image, banner or logo. Pre-header copy should describe in an enticing way, what you're about to talk about or promote. It's important because it's what most recipients will see when your email lands in their inbox, before they've actually physically seen the body of the email you've sent. It looks something like this:

Your Name
Subject
Pre-header copy

All too often I see things like this.

Manor House Hotel
February Newsletter
View as webpage

This example is particularly bad as it uses a terrible subject line, has no personalisation in the name, and there is no pre-header. Those three lines tell me nothing to inspire and intrigue me to stop what I'm doing and pay attention to an email I neither care about nor am interested in. The above, by the way is not uncommon for hotel emails. For all I know, this email could contain the exact deal, in the right location at the right price at the right time that I'm looking for. But I would never know because their unimaginative approach has left me to conclude that their email is not as important as whatever I was doing when it arrived in my inbox.

A much better approach might be something like this:

Jane at Manor House Hotel
Did you see the news, Adam?
February awards and rock-bottom prices

Now *this* email might go on to tell me about some recent awards the hotel has won or been nominated for. It might give me some great, time-sensitive offer to book at the hotel. But with a little personalisation, creativity and a carefully thought-through pre-header, this email is more likely to get opened.

To access my "Quick Start To Successful Email Check List" visit www.moredirectboookings.com/resources

15. DESIGN

Without question, an aesthetically appealing email is preferable to a messy one. The design is important and should provide a well-rounded representation of the property. However, design is such a small part of the sales process, and it should not be given any more time and consideration than it deserves. In my experience, far too much concern, time and effort is placed on making the email look right, and too little time is spent getting the actual text and message right. And yet, when you think about it, it's the words that do the talking, that build and nurture the relationship, that evoke feelings of delight, annoyance and desire. The design, on the other hand, can only influence these important factors for a mere moment. It the email looks great, then the recipient will be encouraged to read on, and similarly if the email looks terrible, the recipient won't be encouraged to read on.

The design of the email is only there to facilitate the achievement of the desired objectives of the email (get it read and get the recipient to take action); it won't get it all done for you.

> With this in mind, at The Cranleigh Boutique, we use a basic template that works for every client. Visit www.moredirectbookings.com/resources to view this template

Using our preferred marketing system Active Campaign, we use a responsive design (meaning that it will automatically adapt to the size of the screen the email is being viewed on i.e. tablet, phone, etc.). We customise for each email and client. The use of the side bar is an important element as it allows us to not only lay out a clear dual readership path but the main body text is kept short in line length and therefore easier to read.

Images within the design are important, and if you feel that you want your email to be image led—then great, but still write the email with a short message with a *dear* and *from* —as if it were a real piece of correspondence between one person and another.

Last point on design is to ensure that your header image is no more than 300 pixels in height and normally 630 pixels in width. What the recipient sees "above the fold" is influential to getting them to the next step of reading and engaging. If the recipient can only see one whopping big image when they open it, your message is more likely to be missed.

16. PLAIN TEXT EMAILS

Emails are sent in two ways—plain text or HTML. HTML emails are the flashy, image-based and trackable ones. Plain text emails will not contain images, won't even allow you to alter the font and you can't use tracking to see which links have been clicked. You might be wondering why anyone would want to send a plain text email. There are two reasons: some email providers will only display plain text emails, (this can normally be changed within the settings) so if you go to a great deal of trouble designing and writing a beautiful marketing email, and don't provide a plain text alternative, chances are you're missing out on people who would have otherwise engaged with your email.

The second reason you might want to send a plain text email is that, frankly, they can seem more genuine. Most marketing emails look exactly like that: marketing emails. So even with the most intriguing subject line, killer offer and most beautifully designed aesthetic, some recipients will just take the stance, "No, I'm not prepared to be marketed to today," and therefore they won't open or read the email. A plain text email however takes a completely different approach. Regularly we prepare an email written from the owner of the hotel, seemingly directly to the recipient as if they had sat there typing away at their keyboard just a few moments ago. Imagine; the owner of this hotel has taken time to personally write to me!

It might seem silly, but believe me it works. We often send a question within these plain text emails, sometimes focusing on the fact that the hotel is trying hard to get things right with their emails, and asking if the recipient finds them annoying, entertaining, too frequent, etc. The feedback is always overwhelming. These plain text emails are used to best effect when you don't sell, by the way. Get some engagement by saying, "Thank you," or by asking for the customer's opinion about something. Show a willingness to improve, and write in a professional but informal tone. I can't stress how important a (seemingly) personal email from someone in authority has on the level of engagement that customer has with the hotel.

To access my "Quick Start To Successful Email Check List" visit www.moredirectbookings.com/resources

17. PS

Final point of any email is the postscript, or the PS. A PS is an effective way of reiterating what you want the customer to do. Whatever action it is, be that 'call to check availability' or 'click this link', etc. reiterate it in the PS because statistically the recipient is more likely to read the PS than any other paragraph or sentence in the bottom half of the email. Remember, skim reading is rife amongst email recipients; you probably do it yourself, and the PS is a clever way to encourage the recipient to understand what it is that you want them to do and get them to do it.

Occasionally we use a PPS too, which is a good way of reiterating a benefit of taking the desired action that you encouraged in your PS. It might look something like this:

PS—Don't delay, these rooms will fill up fast at this rate; call now on [tracking telephone number] to check availability.

PPS—Remember too that the first 50 customers will receive a free bottle of Champagne on ice, waiting in their room. Act now and enjoy a bottle of bubbles on us.

To access my "Quick Start To Successful Email Check List" visit www.moredirectbookings.com/resources

18. HOW TO AVOID SPAM COMPLAINTS

It was mentioned earlier in this section of the book that avoiding spam complaints is a necessity to ensure that your online reputation remains in tact. Well, we have developed a clever way to ensure that if prospective or previous customers no longer wish to hear from us, we can simply have them safely unsubscribe from all further correspondence without the risk of them complaining as spam.

Admittedly it takes a little more work but it's worth it because the average Joe email recipient has no idea of the damage it can do the business if a high volume of spam complaints are received. Equally, the typical recipient of emails will not know the difference between unsubscribing and reporting as spam.

Worse still, when you've taken the trouble to actively ask if the customer is happy to receive email correspondence from your hotel, and they report you as spam on the first email, it's really quite annoying!

So, mini rant over! This is how you over come it. As suggested before, add in an unsubscribe link somewhere prominent on the email – either on the top or the bottom. But, don't use the 'unsubscribe' feature on your CRM. Instead, type the words 'Unsubscribe here' (or something to that effect) and highlight these words, creating a hyperlink. That's step one.

Now go to your website, or ask the person or company who manages your website to create a separate page on your site with the following address:

Yourhotel.com/unsubscribe

On this page, should simply read something along the lines of the following:

UNSUBSCRIBE CONFIRMATION

You are now unsubscribed from all email lists.

That's step two. Now take that unsubscribe web link and link your 'unsubscribe here' email copy to the page that you've just created.

Step three is to review the email statistics 24-36 hours after your broadcast and manually unsubscribe everyone who clicked that link. It's a little more work, but it will safeguard your online reputation and is well worth doing.

Last pointer on this is to drop 5-6 lines of blank space at the bottom of the email. By law, you are required to give each email recipient the opportunity to unsubscribe so most (if not all) CRM systems will add this link in by default at the bottom of the email. So if you drop in your special unsubscribe link just below the end of the main email body, followed by 5-6 lines of blank space before the mandatory unsubscribe link provided by your CRM system, you'll encourage recipients of your email to click your unsubscribe link, that safeguards your online reputation.

> For practical examples of what these spam complaint avoiders look like and how they work, visit www.moredirectbookings.com/resources

PART THREE

REFERRAL POSTCARDS

An often-overlooked area of business is referral bookings—word-of-mouth marketing. A common facet of this type of marketing is that it is haphazard, sporadic and random; if you delivered great service to a customer and they leave the hotel raving about you, you'll hope that they tell a few people and that those people go on to book with you too.

But there's a problem with this approach, and it stems from the word *hope*. What this approach is effectively saying is that whilst you acknowledge that there are only three types of people that stay in your hotel (new, repeat and referred customers) you are doing absolutely nothing to drive this third bunch of customers into the hotel. And in instances where something is done, typically it will be a half-hearted mention in an email with zero follow-up and zero measurement.

Well I'd rather not leave this entire market segment to chance—and our referral postcards seem to work quite well for hotels where the guests are predominantly there for leisure purposes.

This is the simplest marketing system we use. Here's what you do:
1) Get a few thousand postcards printed.
2) Leave 2 or 3 in each room explaining they are complimentary postcards.
3) The customer brings 2 or 3 completed postcards to the front desk and you post them.

Simple. But admittedly there's a bit more to it. On the front of the postcard is a selection of beautiful imagery and the hotel's logo. On the back is a very clear call-to-action advising that you offer a preferred friends and family rates that are only available on this link (normally www.hotelname.com/friends). A tracking telephone number is in place on the postcard and again on the friends' landing page that you plan to drive them to.

The very premise of this "system" is that you are getting your hotel in front of a prospective customer and at the same time word-of-mouth marketing is happening. Your existing guest will write about how lovely a time they're having and how nice the hotel is, right next to a preferred friends and family rate!

Now the cost of the postcard printing will be negligible; we recently spent about £60 on 2,000 postcards. The cost of postage is slightly more expensive at approximately £0.57 in the UK. This is where it becomes crucial to be on top of your numbers, most notably your cost-per-sale. Earlier in the book we used an example of an OTA commission model in which, based on the average booking at £200 and a commission percentage of 15%, we ascertained that the cost-per-sale was £30. So the goal here is to drive business for less than the cost of £30.

So, to make this a worthwhile proposition, i.e. less than £30 cost-per-sale, you'll need to make a booking from approximately 1 in 50 postcards. We're now delivering sales to our hotel clients from about 1 in 15, giving us a cost-per-sale of £8.55. So broadly, for every £30 spent with an OTA, £200 of gross revenue is delivered, but for every £30 spent on referral postcards, over £600 of gross revenue is delivered. That's more than a 200% higher return on the investment.

Sounds lovely and (hopefully) straight forward, but there's an element of expectation management needed here. Sure in the above example, you're over 200% better off, but the referral postcard "system" doesn't bring volume anywhere near what the top OTAs do. The referral postcard system for our best performing hotels delivers 10 or 15 bookings a month. To expect that this one system will overtake the OTAs is unrealistic, but it's a start. There is no magic bullet to driving more direct business, no one thing that will do all the work for you, but the referral postcard system is a typical example of one thing your hotel can do to maximise profitable sales. When you have 5, 10 or 20 of these little systems delivering, you can gain an extra 10-15 bookings per month, and a noticeable difference can be made to your profitability.

For examples of some of the successful referral postcards we've created, visit www.moredirectbookings.com/resources

THE COMPLETE HOTEL MARKETING SYSTEM

Online marketing moves fast, and typically hotels are slow to react. It's no wonder websites like Booking.com enjoy the success they do; some whizzy techy kids at some point in the early 2000's cottoned on to the fact that not only do consumers love comparisons, but there are quite literally hundreds of thousands of hotels in the world that demand incredible amounts of time from the hoteliers who run them, and these people simply do not have the time (let alone the inclination) to market their businesses effectively. Thus, this online commission model soon came into its own and nowadays I don't meet a single hotelier who doesn't want more direct business and less commission to pay, but by the same token, I can count on one hand the amount of hoteliers I've met who actually know what to do (and importantly; what not to do) to grow their direct bookings. And even fewer are prepared to work at marketing the business themselves.

And so what typically happens is one of three things:

1. No marketing actually gets done. Maybe there is an adhoc, haphazard advertisement somewhere that may or may not deliver new bookings, but the majority of the business is completely and utterly dependent on throwing up a website, sticking your inventory on the OTAs and hoping that the phone rings!

2. The hotel has sufficient turnover and profit to hire a marketing person. This allows the owner or the manager to focus on keeping customers happy and making sure the hotel runs smoothly, etc. The common problem with this approach is that this marketing person focuses

on brand marketing—all the fluffy stuff that you think you should do to promote the hotel, but there's zero accountability. This person sends out email newsletters, buys advertising space in local magazines, posts on Facebook and Twitter, and other such noise. Generally, these people have no idea where their bookings are coming from and no idea if what they spend their time doing is delivering more direct bookings.

3. The owner or manager attempts to manage the marketing themselves but inevitably fails to give sufficient time and effort to learning how to market effectively enough to make the time, money and effort a better solution that using OTAs. These are the types of people that spend an hour or two setting up Google Adwords, lose £500 in a week and never touch it again. Or they send a sales email to a cold list which gets dozens of spam complaints with zero sales and claim email marketing doesn't work for their hotel.

If you found yourself nodding at one of these three types of scenarios, this next marketing system will make all the difference. It works best when you have absolute clarity on who it is you're wanting to target, and what it is that you want to sell them. So let's say you want to target more engaged women for your wedding packages or more 50+ couples for your midweek breaks, or maybe you've noticed a trend of golfers coming to stay and play at nearby courses and find that these types of customers are worth pursuing. Whatever it is and whoever you want to target is irrelevant; going through the process of identifying a particular group, however, is essential.

You start by targeting using online advertising platforms. Earlier in the book we discussed Facebook Ads and Google Adwords. My preference is Facebook Ads because the accuracy of targeting is typically higher and the cost-per-click can be as much as 100 times lower. Let's take the example of golfers.

Using Facebook Ads, you might decide to target using the following criteria:
- Men
- Aged 35-65
- Interested in golf
- Within a 50-mile radius of 3 affluent towns no more than a 2-hour drive away from the hotel

These ads will drive users to a landing page. Now this landing page is specific to golfers and the information shares all the reasons why your hotel is the ideal base for golfers. The key is relevance. Ads must be relevant to the landing page, and relevant to the package you're selling. Now once they are on this landing page, there are only three things that prospective customers can do. These are:

1. Enquire over the phone or make an online booking

In this case it's job done: you've managed to get them to take significant action and a meaningful step toward becoming a customer, pending the formality of actually going through the reservation process.

2. Subscribe

Via some kind of lead-magnet, or incentive offer, you capture the information of the prospective customer so you can market to them on an on-going basis until they eventually become a customer.

3. Leave the landing page

This will happen. In which case, golf-specific Google Remarketing ads will follow them around for a period of 30 days (or however long you choose) so that you can encourage them to come back to the site and hopefully take action 1 or 2.

> A diagram and working example of this marketing system is available by visiting www.moredirectbookings.com/resources

Now, when the prospective customer takes actions 1 or 3, there's little more to do, but when they subscribe, the automation systems kick in—namely auto-responding emails and lead-scoring automation.

Let's stick to the golfing example. Perhaps the lead-magnet you use to encourage the subscription offers 25% off green fees at local courses, or maybe you offer 10 tips to improving your golf swing in a handy downloadable PDF. Naturally I'd recommend testing different lead-magnets to see what converts best. So they've subscribed, and this triggers a set of auto-responding emails, each one driving the prospective customer back to the website. The lead-scoring automation will measure engagement by email reads and clicks plus website views. You then set notifications to particular members of the team when a prospective customer hits perhaps 7-10 lead scoring points within a 24-hour period. If it's a wedding or corporate system, you might want members of the team to call these individuals when they are showing significant levels of engagement i.e., 7-10 points within a 24-hour period. Or you might want to automate a pro-active approach by sending a personal email to the engaged prospective customer that reads something like this . . .

Dear [firstname]

{yourname} here, the General Manager of {hotel name}. I hope you don't mind my getting in touch, but I noticed that not long ago you downloaded {lead-magnet} but having looked through our recent bookings, we don't seem to have received one from you recently.

Are you perhaps still thinking about it? Or maybe you're weighing your options still.

Well my team and I would be delighted to welcome you to {hotel name} and as an extra incentive to stay, I've briefed the team to offer you an extra 10% off if you book within the next 24 hours.

Just call {tracking number} and one of my team on the front desk will be looking forward to receiving your call and getting you booked in.

With kindest regards,
{your name}

Now you don't have to go with an incentive, and you don't have to give another 10% off, but the process of pro-actively reaching out to a prospective customer to capture their business, and sweetening the deal with a little something extra if they book before a certain deadline might get them off the fence and into one of your hotel rooms. These systems work because they run automatically and you lose nothing if they don't book!

This "Complete Marketing System" as I refer to it has made our hotels thousands from very small marketing budgets. It is not uncommon for us to capture subscribers for less than a £1 and sales for less than £5. And when you use this system in a wedding context, the numbers get even more exciting. From £100 spent at the top of the system, we've added over £20,000 in wedding sales to hotels. Provided you've got the right follow-up and sales procedures in place, this marketing system can provide you with enough prospective customers and enquiries to grow any side of your business.

> Full information on how to get this system working for you, including a step-by-step guide for getting started, can be found at www.moredirectbookings.com/resources

SUMMARY & CONCLUSION

In this book, I have laid out almost everything I know about how to market a hotel to achieve more direct business. These systems, tools and strategies have helped my own hotel, The Cranleigh Boutique to achieve over 96% direct business and dozens more hotels to significantly reduce dependency on the OTAs.

You would have done well not to notice that the resources page on this book's website (www.moredirectbookings.com/resources) is a highly recommended resource. Within that resource, I've created dozens of step-by-step videos, templates and how-to guides to ensure you have everything you need to make a meaningful difference to the amount of direct bookings your hotel can attract.

Hopefully what's come across through these pages is that my team and I have worked hard over these last few years to understand why and how customers book hotels. By adopting a near obsessive desire to learn and implement the things that work to drive more profitable, zero-commission bookings, it's changed not only my life, but the lives of my family, my staff and the overall experience we can offer to our customers.

As I write this in 2015, there is a massive problem in our industry. The OTAs have walked in and taken over. The companies making the most money in our industry are no longer the super luxury hotel groups, it's the agents; forcing the independent hotelier to be left behind. It is my belief that the strategies provided in this book, and the extra done-for-you guides provided on moredirectbookings.com/resources will change all of that. I sincerely hope you take the initiative to put into action these strategies and are able to achieve the same level of direct bookings success that we have enjoyed at The Cranleigh Boutique these last few years, and that the hotels whom we supply done for you marketing services for have also enjoyed.

Good luck to you and your hotel, and let's beat those OTAs together. Thank you for reading.

Printed in Great Britain
by Amazon